OUR STORIES, OUR VOICES

OUR STORIES, OUR VOICES

21 YA AUTHORS GET REAL ABOUT INJUSTICE, EMPOWERMENT, AND GROWING UP FEMALE IN AMERICA

EDITED BY AMY REED

SIMON PULSE

NEW YORK · LONDON · TORONTO · SYDNEY · NEW DELHI

Certain names and characteristics have been changed.

SIMON PULSE

An imprint of Simon & Schuster Children's Publishing Division
1230 Avenue of the Americas, New York, New York 10020
First Simon Pulse hardcover edition August 2018
Compilation copyright © 2018 by Amy Reed
"My Immigrant American Dream" copyright © 2018 by Sandhya Menon; "Her Hair
Was Not of Gold" copyright © 2018 by Anna-Marie McLemore; "Finding My Feminism"
copyright © 2018 by Amy Reed; "Unexpected Pursuits: Embracing My Indigeneity & Creativity"
copyright © 2018 by Christine Day; "Chilled Monkey Brains" copyright © 2018 by Sona Charaipotra;
"Roar" copyright © 2018 by Jaye Robin Brown; "Easter Offering" copyright © 2018 by
Brandy Colbert; "Trumps and Trunchbulls" copyright © 2018 by Alexandra Duncan;
"Tiny Battles" copyright © 2018 by Maurene Goo; "These Words Are Mine" copyright © 2018 by
Stephanie Kuehnert; "Fat and Loud" copyright © 2018 by Julie Murphy; "Myth Making: In the Wake
of Hardship" copyright © 2018 by Somaiya Daud; "Changing Constellations" copyright © 2018
by Nina LaCour; "The One Who Defines Me" copyright © 2018 by Aisha Saeed; "In Our
Genes" copyright © 2018 by Hannah Moskowitz; "An Accidental Activist" copyright © 2018 by
Ellen Hopkins; "Dreams Deferred and Other Explosions" copyright © 2018 by Ilene (I.W.) Gregorio;
"Not Like the Other Girls" copyright © 2018 by Martha Brockenbrough; "Is Something
Bothering You?" copyright © 2018 by Jenny Torres Sanchez; "What I've Learned About Silence"
copyright © 2018 by Amber Smith; "Black Girl, Becoming" copyright © 2018 by Tracy Deonn Walker
Jacket illustration copyright © 2018 by Mallory Heyer
All rights reserved, including the right of reproduction in whole or in part in any form.
SIMON PULSE and colophon are registered trademarks of Simon & Schuster, Inc.
For information about special discounts for bulk purchases, please contact
Simon & Schuster Special Sales at 1-866-506-1949 or business@simonandschuster.com.
The Simon & Schuster Speakers Bureau can bring authors to your live event.
For more information or to book an event contact the Simon & Schuster Speakers
Bureau at 1-866-248-3049 or visit our website at www.simonspeakers.com.
Jacket designed by Heather Palisi
Interior designed by Mike Rosamilia
The text of this book was set in Palatino.
Manufactured in the United States of America
2 4 6 8 10 9 7 5 3 1
Library of Congress Cataloging-in-Publication Data
Names: Reed, Amy Lynn editor.
Title: Our stories, our voices : 21 YA authors get real about injustice, empowerment,
and growing up female in America / edited by Amy Reed.
Description: First Simon Pulse hardcover edition. | New York : Simon Pulse, 2018.
Identifiers: LCCN 2017029042 (print) | LCCN 2017042250 (eBook) |
ISBN 9781534409019 (eBook) | ISBN 9781534408999 (hardcover)
Subjects: LCSH: Young women—United States—Social conditions—21st century. |
Equality—United States. | Feminism—United States.
Classification: LCC HQ799.7 (eBook) | LCC HQ799.7 .O925 2018 (print) |
DDC 305.420973/0905—dc23
LC record available at https://lccn.loc.gov/2017029042

FOR ALL OF US WHO AT TIMES
FEEL LOST AND POWERLESS.
MAY WE CONTINUE TO FIND,
AND FIGHT FOR, OURSELVES
AND ONE ANOTHER.

CONTENTS

INTRODUCTION
Amy Reed

In the days after the 2016 presidential election, I felt lost.

Like so many people, I was overwhelmed by feelings of shock and powerlessness. I needed a way out of my despair; I needed to *do* something. So I became determined to channel those feelings into action and hope. Out of that determination, and the determination of twenty other YA authors to make our voices heard, this book was born.

No matter where your beliefs fall on the political spectrum, or even if you don't consider yourself political at all, it is impossible to deny that we are living in a time when many people are afraid. Many people are angry. Hate and fear seem to be the ruling emotions in our country. I've had countless conversations with people who are terrified by what seem to be the very real possibilities of nuclear war, the mass deportation of millions of immigrants, the overturning of *Roe v. Wade* and marriage equality, the government's open support of white supremacy, homophobia, transphobia, Islamophobia, xenophobia, ableism, sexism, and racism. I keep hearing stories of emboldened hatred and violence, of kids being bullied in school and nobody stopping it, of trans kids committing suicide. I know so many survivors of sexual assault and abuse whose trauma is being triggered by the behavior and rhetoric of those in power. We are living in a cultural battleground where, for many of us, our very identities seem to be under attack.

My heart hurts. I have a four-year-old daughter who deserves a better world than this. You deserve a better world than this. So I asked myself: *How can I help? How can I be part of the solution? What is my power and how can I use it?*

My power is in my words, in storytelling. I knew I had a story to tell. I knew my friends, the incredible YA authors in this collection, all had stories to tell. I thought of you—young people across the country who may be feeling scared and threatened, with your own stories that need to be told and heard. I wanted to do something to help you know you're not alone in your fear and anger, to help you know that your stories—your *lives*—are valid, and valued. So many of us are hearing the message right now that we do not belong, that we are not welcome. To that—I think I speak on behalf of all the authors in this book—I say bullshit. You are wanted. You are loved. You belong. I hope you read these pages and see yourself in our stories, see that there is a place for you, with us. I hope the words of these authors help you feel less alone. I hope you read about women just like you, and I hope you read about women very different from you, and I hope that your heart opens for all of them. I hope you see in the diversity of our stories a common light, a shared humanity and dignity, a community that includes you and the people you care about.

Telling our stories, speaking our truths, is in itself an act of resistance. Ours are the stories many in power seem to think do not matter. Ours are the marginalized voices they refuse to listen to. This book, this act of resistance, says our stories matter. Our lives matter. Our voices will not be silenced.

The women in these pages are daughters and sisters and partners and mothers. We are young and not so young. We are scared and brave and sad and full of joy. We are not perfect. We are works in progress, still growing, still healing. We are survivors of abuse and hate and sexual assault. We are immigrants. We are Christians and Muslims and Jews and Hindus and agnostics. We are American Indian and Indian-American. We are white and Black and Asian and Latina. We are so many shades of brown. We are straight and queer. I regret that there are no trans writers in this collection, but please know, if you are trans or gender nonconforming, we hold a place for you, too.

In this collection, you will read stories of hope and empowerment. You will read about healing and self-discovery. You will read about love, family, and community. You will read about courage and activism. But many of the stories are not so obviously optimistic. Some of them may be very difficult to read. Many of us have been victims of hate and racism. Some of us have been raped. Many of us spent our teen years confused and lost and angry. Some of us still feel confused and lost and angry. Some of us still feel like we live on the margins, that our identities don't quite fit in anywhere. Some of us struggled with writing these essays, struggled with finding a message of hope hiding beneath our fear and pain.

But there is one thing we all have in common: we are all still here. We are speaking out. We are refusing to be silent. Whatever is contained in our stories, what matters most is that we are telling them.

This book is about us. It is about our diverse experiences as women in this country. It is about our vulnerability and strength, our joy and pain, our fear and love. It is about our resilience. It is about our humanity. It is about us getting real. It is about us refusing to be silent. Our stories are our resistance.

This is our love letter to America, to the young people who are hurting and scared. You are not alone. We hear you. We are listening. We stand by you. We will survive as we have always survived: together.

This book is dedicated to all the women and all the girls, to our trans and nonbinary siblings, to the men and boys who stand as our allies, to everyone who cares about building a home for justice.

Keep speaking your truth. Keep telling your story. The world needs your voice, now more than ever.

EDITOR'S NOTE

Dear Reader,

Some of the essays in this collection deal with sensitive subject matter that may be disturbing, traumatizing, or triggering for certain readers.

If you are sensitive to stories of abuse and sexual assault, you may want to take extra care with the following essays:

"What I've Learned about Silence" by Amber Smith

"Trumps and Trunchbulls" by Alexandra Duncan

"These Words Are Mine" by Stephanie Kuehnert

"Not Like Other Girls" by Martha Brockenbrough

"Finding My Feminism" by Amy Reed

If you are sensitive to portrayals of racist violence, you may want to take extra care with the following essays:

"Easter Offering" by Brandy Colbert

"Chilled Monkey Brains" by Sona Charaipotra

"The One Who Defines Me" by Aisha Saeed

"Is Something Bothering You?" by Jenny Torres Sanchez

With love,

Amy Reed

OUR STORIES, OUR VOICES

MY IMMIGRANT AMERICAN DREAM

Sandhya Menon

My first night in America was a sleepless one spent wide-eyed in the dark, listening to the crushing silence. *This is going to be great,* I promised my fifteen-year-old self. *You're going to love it here.*

My family and I had just moved to Charleston, South Carolina, from Mumbai (Bombay), India. We'd moved periodically between India and the United Arab Emirates before, but I'd always lived an insulated life in the Middle East, studying at Indian schools and engaging mainly with the very large Indian community there. This, being plunged into a brand-new culture in a brand-new country where the population of Indians wasn't nearly as numerous, was completely novel. The lack of noisy, bustling rickshaws and street vendors hawking glass bangles and multicolored saris would take some getting used to. But the thing I had to get used to the most was being an outsider in a country of outsiders.

I'd heard from excited friends and relatives that America was the land of immigrants. "Even the white people who are the majority there are actually immigrants, if you look at their ancestors!" people told me. "Plus, Americans love people who are different. Just look at San Francisco." We knew many friends who had immigrated to America, whose children were born there, and the stories that trickled home were dotted with details that made me salivate: convertible cars and spotless beaches, people who dressed like Westerners in short-shorts and tank tops. Besides, America was famous for its equal treatment of women. India still had huge strides to make in that arena when I lived there, and I was eager for a change. I was *so* ready to be welcomed with open arms, to make exotic American friends who might grow to love Bollywood movies and Hindi songs like I did.

What happened was a little less idyllic. I had a thick Indian accent when I first moved to the States, and people—including some teachers at my small magnet school—immediately thought that meant I couldn't speak English, period. By then I'd already had short stories (written in English) published in international magazines, so that wasn't the case at all. There were also other micro- and macroaggressions to get used to, ones I wasn't expecting from the land of immigrants.

I distinctly remember my father speaking to store clerks

who would sigh and roll their eyes because they couldn't understand him. They spoke slowly and loudly, as if *he*—a highly educated engineer who'd lived all over the world— were having trouble understanding *them*. Occasionally I was stopped in my neighborhood by the police and asked what I was doing there, whether I was in the country legally, and where I lived. As far as I could tell, the only reason I was stopped was because of the color of my skin. My friend who'd emigrated from Russia the same year as me reported never having experienced that particular form of harassment. One boy insisted on sneeringly calling me Ganesh in class because of the religion my parents practiced, and the teacher never stepped in. At the post office someone yelled at me and my mom to go back to our country because, apparently, we were standing in line wrong. I got used to the question, asked seemingly casually but with a gimlet eye: "Are you here *legally*?" whenever I said I didn't have a social security number, since I was here as a dependent on my dad's work visa. It made my cheeks burn at first. My parents had paid a lot of money to come to the States; we'd gone through all the proper channels and jumped through all the hoops (and of those there were many). What right did they have to ask me that when they didn't even know how visas worked, when many of them had never even been out of this country? And anyway, what did they think? That I swam all the way from India?

Not all experiences were negative, however. I did enjoy

greater gender equality in the United States than I had in India. Egalitarian messages pervaded my high school: we were told we could do anything a boy could do, be anything a boy could be. Still, these messages were implicitly and explicitly targeted at white girls and women. The role models and those they spoke to looked nothing like me.

For the longest time I thought there must be something wrong with *me* for people—even people I respected or considered my friends—to say the things I was hearing. Once I realized I *was* accepted as a woman, just not as an immigrant, I figured I needed to acculturate better. The other Indian kids around me, the ones who seemed to be accepted, at least to my eye, seemed indistinguishable in accent and dress from the American kids. (At the time I didn't get the concept of Indian-Americanness.) So I began to speak with an American accent. I tried to blend in so much that I would actively decry Indian things. When people asked me about arranged marriage I would announce that I didn't believe in it. When people asked if I spoke Hindi, I automatically said, "Yes, but I speak English better and it was my first language." I began to shop at Old Navy whenever my parents would let me, and I relegated all my Indian clothes to the back of my closet.

One of the biggest losses, though, was my art. Although I still wrote in a private journal, my stories and drawings began to go by the wayside. I refused to let people peek into my imagination. I didn't know what was "acceptable" anymore, so I simply stopped creating. I was, without thinking, trying to obliterate those parts of myself that I thought weren't American enough (and to me, in those days, "American" meant "white" because that's the message I was getting). I wanted to be lighter skinned, taller. I wanted to blend in and become someone else. I was trying to perfect the art of becoming the human chameleon.

But as I went through high school and then college, a strange and wonderful thing started to happen. I began to see myself for who I was, past all the cladding of "immigrant versus American born," of "accent versus no accent." There was a side to me, I realized, that had nothing to do with the labels other people gave me. I started to pay attention to that side more, to unearth who I was for myself.

My volunteering with the teen crisis line and individuals with developmental disabilities, for instance, helped me see I was a person capable of empathy and kindness. My high school best friend, who happened to be the daughter of Nigerian immigrants, helped me see that there was nothing inherently wrong with being an immigrant. She embraced her Nigerian roots and celebrated her parents' accent and where they'd come from. The way she spoke openly about the injustices they faced helped me see that that's what they were—injustices, prejudice, ignorance. I'd had a hard time seeing it when it was directed at me, but seeing it directed at a friend drew the line between right and wrong pretty starkly.

I met incredible women in the places where I volunteered,

who told stories of overcoming traumatic pasts and abusive partners, mental illness and poverty. We had a mutual sense of responsibility to share what resources we now had with others less fortunate. We spoke about what it meant to be female, how easy it was to be hurt, but how capable we were of healing.

I enjoyed the freedom of being able to walk down the street without being incessantly catcalled or waiting in line without being groped. I began to see that I had inherent worth as a young woman that went beyond my looks, and I was eager to see what that might look like for me.

Although my high school teachers had not seen much merit in my writing, people at college did. I still remember one of my English professors telling me he'd seen my essay in the literary magazine. He looked at me appraisingly from behind his glasses. "You're a good writer," he said. "Have you written anything else?" And so I began to believe, once again, that I was talented, that I had something to offer that other people wanted to see. I met my husband, a white boy, who believed that I was beautiful as I was—dark skinned, on the shorter side, with curly black hair.

I began to realize that for every ignorant, misinformed, or prejudiced person I met, there was a counterbalancing person in the world who would recognize my worth and stand up for me and others like me. I heard the Mr. Rogers quote, "When I was a boy and I would see scary things in the news, my mother would say to me, 'Look for the helpers. You will always find people who are helping,'" and it really resonated with me. It was true, I realized. And somehow, realizing that other, *good* people saw me as worthy helped me realize that people who didn't see my worth, who automatically categorized me as "less than," were the ones in the wrong. I had to lean on other people to find myself, but once I did, I began to blossom.

It was a little like emerging after hibernation, I imagine. I came out into the sunlight, blinking and unsteady, but I was warm again. I began to tunnel my way out of self-doubt and anxiety. I realized I was so much happier when I put myself in charge of my life, when I refused to accept what other, misinformed people said about me. A large part of that, too, was realizing that adults weren't always right. Being raised in Indian culture, I'd been taught to always respect my elders, to never disagree, to accept what I was told. But adults, I was quickly learning, could be judgmental and cruel, prejudiced and bigoted. Adults did not automatically get a pass anymore. I had a right to question them.

I began to make art again, with gusto. I drew, painted, and wrote short stories and poems. I sometimes even made up song lyrics and music, though I'd never considered myself especially musically gifted. It was at this time that I began to realize that I had a voice and I could use it to tell my story. Who cared if it wasn't perfect? I knew there must be people out there who experienced the same things I did—the cold pain of otherness, the sting of rejection, the joy of connection, the particular pain and beauty of being a woman, the brilliant and ecstatic freedom of creating—regardless of their backgrounds. I thought about the stories I'd read that had touched me, from people like Enid Blyton and Kate Chopin, women whom I had little in common with on the surface. Still, I'd recognized parts of myself in their stories. Art, for me, though I didn't think about it in concrete terms then, was about pushing against all the hands that swatted me back down when I tried to grasp for the American dream. It was my way of saying, *I belong just as much as you do. I'm here to stay.*

Little by little, by first claiming my femaleness, I also began to reclaim my Indianness. It hadn't been totally discarded, I happily found, just lying dormant, a seed waiting for sunshine and air. I stopped providing disclaimers about arranged marriage and my ability to speak Hindi. But more than that, I began to talk about my time in India, to really relish telling people how things were different where I had spent a significant part of my childhood. I began to understand that being Indian was just different from being American, no better and no worse. Moving to the States at fifteen certainly changed some parts of me. As an Indian-American, I prize financial independence and ambition more than most of the female elders in my family did when I was growing up. I'm also much more liberal about social issues. At the same time, though, I've retained the collectivistic attitude of the importance of family. Although I don't see elders as infallible anymore, I do still believe in the wisdom of the ages.

I don't view myself as a chameleon now, but rather as a tree, constantly adding new branches and leaves, growing and turning purposefully to the sun. There's so much more to life, I feel, than trying to shoehorn yourself into one identity, one way of being. What authority says, anyway, that you have to be one thing or the other, that you can't successfully straddle more than one self? There may be people out there, especially in this tumultuous political climate, who are vocal about this: you can be *either* American or an immigrant, you can *either* speak with an accent or speak the "right" way, you can *either* be female on our terms or accept the label we give you, you can *either* assimilate completely or get out. To them I say respectfully, you're missing the point of America. Perhaps one of the most important lessons I've learned in my nearly twenty years in this wonderful country is this: there is no one way to be American. There is no one language, no one color, no one accent, no one religion. We are a country of multitudes; we should be proud to remain that way.

I am still learning. I'd be lying if I said it didn't still sting when people shouted insults at me. I was recently at a protest where I felt that cold, heavy ache of otherness as people chanted and jeered at me and people like me, as they told me to go back to my country, as they refused to accept my right to live alongside them simply because of the color of my skin and where I was born. I still have days when the fight feels never ending, when I wonder if I will ever be able to exist without having to justify my existence.

But on those days I look to the helpers and to others like me. On those days, most importantly, I look inside myself.

I give myself permission to be exactly who I am, where I am. I give myself permission to participate fully in the American dream. I am still learning, but I am starting to accept that this is the only permission I need.

HER HAIR WAS NOT OF GOLD

Anna-Marie McLemore

I have a theory:

Every theater geek has their own theater dream. Maybe it's restaging *Cinderella* in the 1920s. Or redesigning the costumes for the dance of the Sugar Plum Fairy. Or being the first genderqueer actor cast as the Emcee in a national production of *Cabaret*. (Just three of the ones I've heard.)

In my teens, mine was probably either a role in the ensemble of *Riverdance,* or getting to design an elaborate lighting concept for a friend's original script (in case you're wondering: tendonitis, and we never quite found the budget for that production).

But before that, in grade school, I had a dream role. And it wasn't Juliet or Velma Kelly or even the Lilac Fairy in *Sleeping Beauty*.

It was the Virgin Mary.

Since the first Christmas pageant I ever saw, I wanted to kneel in front of that manger with my head bowed, playing the girl I admired most. A girl I'd read about in the Bible for as long as I could read. I wanted to wear the blue cloth that signaled her purity and loyalty of heart. (A few years later, when a history-obsessed friend told me how expensive blue cloth had been before modern dye processes, I would wonder how la Virgen had come by it. Had the angels brought it to her? The wise men?)

When I was old enough, and when I heard there might be a Christmas pageant I could audition for, I got up the courage to tell a teacher I wanted to try for it.

She laughed.

Not cruelly.

More like I'd made a charming joke, the kind of thing adults like to quote children saying and then laugh over.

"Oh, honey," the teacher said. "Do you really think you're right for the part?"

Was it because I was too short?

Was it because I still had some of what my *tías* called my baby fat? There was a white girl who liked to poke my stomach and tell me how I'd never be pretty because I'd always look like a little girl. (This same girl would later get a school award for Christian kindness. I learned early that if you had blond hair and blue eyes and a sweet smile and just the right number of freckles, there was much the world would give you.)

But then, as I looked around at the posters and Bible illustrations and nativity figurines, a dim idea of what the teacher meant buzzed around me like a mosquito. I noticed something I had faintly registered before but was really looking at for the first time.

They were all blond.

The Marys around me were all blond.

Whether she was praying her song or journeying to Bethlehem beneath Christ's star, Mary was always blond. In the prints where she bowed her head, her hair glowed as a seam of gold beneath her blue veil. And when her eyes were open, when they widened with the wonder of seeing the angels, they were two flecks of brilliant blue.

The Jesuses, too. In paintings of Him praying. In drawings of Him being baptized by John, a dove on his shoulder. Even in nativities where there was enough of the baby's hair grown in to suggest the color. He was always blond.

Except, somehow, when He was on the cross.

Only in the moment of His deepest suffering did artists consider He might have walked this earth as a dark-haired, brown-skinned man. (In depictions of His resurrection and His reappearing, on the other hand, He is shown, as though by magic, blond again.)

I was not right to play la Virgen not because I was too young, or too short, or even because of my baby fat.

I could not be Mary because I did not have the right colors.

I thought this, even as I was surrounded by the godly women

13

of color in my family and my community. I was not *good* like them, I thought. I did not have their sacred hearts.

They were good, but I had to be made good. And I wished and prayed with everything in me for God to make me a girl blue-eyed and blond enough that I could not only play Mary in a Christmas pageant but could grow to have a heart like hers.

If I wanted to be good, I would have to work against my own colors, the ones that teacher had laughed at. If I did this, I thought, I could grow up to be the kind of Christian woman and Christian wife I dreamed of being one day.

Christian wife.

Those two words seemed like two things I could aspire to, no matter what color I was. They seemed clean, uncomplicated.

At least they did until I realized that my heart was different from those girls' at school in more ways than I ever knew.

As a teen I fell in love with a boy who had been assigned female at birth, a boy who would later transition to living the gender expression that was true to him, not the one the world told him to live.

I loved him. I saw this transgender boy as a child of God.

But I couldn't give myself the same grace. My queerness only added to the distance I felt from God, distance born that day I first prayed to be a girl painted in golds and blues.

I didn't speak of those paintings and figurines I'd seen growing up, with their luminous yellow hair and their eyes that looked like drops of the ocean. I didn't speak of the moment when I had realized that the light off their halos was not enough, that the gold had to grow from their heads too.

So I don't know how that boy knew.

But one day, no warning, he asked, "You know Jesus wasn't really a white guy, right?"

I looked at him. We'd been drinking beer we were too young to have on a roof we weren't supposed to be on, watching the kind of Los Angeles sunset that comes in violet and gold and gray. It had been a rare moment of quiet with us, watching that sky. I liked him so much that when he didn't talk, I almost always would, too nervous to let the space between us grow silent.

For him to break that quiet was as rare as a rainstorm over the city.

"What?" I asked.

"I know it's the way all those Renaissance painters show Him, but He wasn't," the boy said.

He had the grace to pretend he was just discussing a fact of history or science, something I might be interested in but not a thing that had plagued me for years.

"Weird, isn't it?" he asked, still watching the sunset, taking a swallow from the bottle and then handing it to me. "We see all those paintings and we take it as some kind of fact that he was white even though it makes no sense."

I nodded, like I'd already known all that and we were just making conversation. I would not admit my ignorance to a boy I liked this much. I had kissed this boy on lighting scaffolds. He had snuck me after hours into the dark theaters where he worked. Still, I had never told him about the role I'd wanted most growing up.

But then I did some research. I looked up articles. I took out books from the library. And I came to understand the distance between the story those paintings and nativity figurines told and the historical Jesus who lived on this earth.

Jesus had dark hair and brown skin.

He was a dark-haired, brown-skinned boy at His birth and during His youth. He was a dark-haired, brown-skinned man during His time as a teacher, during His baptism, at His death, and in His resurrection.

He was a dark-haired, brown-skinned man, not just in His death and suffering, but in His life and His glory.

He was no more like those pictures than the boy I loved was like the cis male husband I once thought I was supposed to have.

It would take a long time to accept myself as the queer Latina girl I was. It would take a long time for me to forget the sound of that teacher's laugh, or to let go of my instinct to believe that saints were spun out of blue and gold. But recognizing two men as they were—embracing my love for a transgender boy, and my reverence for a brown-skinned Jesus—left a seed in me that would grow roots in the years after.

It let me see la Virgen de Guadalupe as she appeared to Juan Diego, her arms full of roses. Juan Diego was a brown-skinned man, and la Virgen told him, as many times as he needed to hear it, that he was a child of God. She showed him in so many flowers, blooming impossibly out of season, that his tilma could barely hold them.

It let me understand myself as a child of God, including, not in spite of, who I was. And it made me sure that no one else—not teachers, not painters, not the world—gets to draw the boundaries of where God's light reaches.

My mother and father worried that facing the world as I am would destroy the faith in me. It almost did. I heard, over and over, *You are too different; we do not want you.* I heard it from those who tried to tell me God would not love me as I was, and I heard it from those who tried to tell me there was no God. But the faith I learned from my mother and father, and from my whole family, stayed with me when the world yelled the things those nativity figurines had whispered.

My husband and I now attend a church that welcomes anyone who draws near the light its stained-glass windows cast on the sidewalks. I love my church home. I love their accepting spirits and their open hearts.

But the pull toward the kind of churches I once knew has never quite left me. Even knowing they wouldn't accept me or my husband, I still feel it.

Sometimes I find myself at the steps of those churches, knowing a little of my heart is just inside the doors. Because even if the church I'm waiting outside may never welcome me, there are others like me.

Maybe I can't change what would happen if we crossed the

threshold into those churches. But sometimes, finding those who are like you, exchanging those looks of *You too?* is enough. It helps us understand that we are not alone. That together we can find church communities that will welcome us as God welcomes us. That yes, maybe a little of our hearts will always be just inside those doors, but God is the one who gave us those hearts.

They are ours to take with us.

FINDING MY FEMINISM

Amy Reed

Here are the things I want you to know about my teen years:

> I was a misfit by choice. I wore weird clothes and didn't shave my armpits. I was way too cool for high school.
>
> I yelled at boys in the hall for saying "faggot."
>
> I got straight As effortlessly.
>
> I went to eight Ani DiFranco concerts by the time I was eighteen.
>
> I was an activist. I went to protests. I planned protests. I wrote press releases for the protests I planned. I marched in the Seattle Pride Parade and Take Back the Night marches. I was interviewed on a public access talk show as an expert on youth rights

activism. I was in the newspaper. I traveled to youth activism conferences in San Francisco and Massachusetts. I was invited to speak at an ACLU convention and got a standing ovation for my speech.

I was hot shit.

Here's what I don't want you to know:

My strength was an illusion.

My empowerment was an illusion.

My thorns were an illusion.

I built a wall of armor around myself because I was
   so soft inside.

I yelled and screamed about the rights of others because
   I could not speak up for myself.

I was not a good feminist.

Don't get me wrong. I cared deeply about all the things I protested: the involuntary commitment of kids to institutions, gay conversion therapy, the corrupt pharmaceutical industry and the overmedication of children, the suspension of a local middle school boy for wearing a skirt to school (though we later discovered it was not an expression of his gender identity but a prank by the class clown). I cared about all the issues I fought for. But there was something else, something hiding beneath all that fighting:

Shame.

* * *

As a teen, these were (I thought) the rules of white, middle-class, midnineties feminism in Seattle:

> Don't wear makeup. Don't shave. Don't be a girly-girl.
> If you sleep with a lot of guys, you're a slut.
> If you sleep with a lot of girls, you're cool.
> The more outspoken and confrontational you are, the
>   better. Your strength is in your thorns.
> Don't show weakness. The worst thing you can ever do
>   is be vulnerable.
> Your greatest strength is in how loud you can say "NO!"

Here's my dirty little secret: I did not know how to say no.

Hiding behind all my posturing and empowerment, all my bristly fake confidence, all the Take Back the Night marches and loud feminism, I felt the secret shame that I was an imposter. Despite all my talk about strength and consent, I held the secret that I felt weak, that so much of who I thought I was had been defined by experiences I did not consent to, how I felt deep down that it was my fault. I shouted "No! No! No!" with my fist pumped in the air, surrounded by an army of strong women, but the truth was I had never been able to say no in my own life when it mattered most. I thought if all those women knew how weak I really was, they would kick me out of feminism.

As I marched through the streets of Seattle chanting about

women uniting and taking back the night, I did not think I was marching for girls like me. My definition of rape and sexual assault was limited to violent attacks by strangers in dark alleys; it was premeditated drugging by crazed, malicious predators. No one I knew was talking about the murky gray area of consent and coercion. No one was talking about me.

I remember secretly wishing we were marching for me. I remember wishing I had earned the right to these women's outrage.

This is my truth: In the shadows of my trauma, shame, and silence, I mistook the misogyny of self-hatred for feminism. I found a way to twist messages of empowerment into oppression. If feminism was about questioning traditional gender roles, then I had to hate everything about myself that was traditionally feminine. If it was about rejecting the idea that a girl's worth is defined by a boy's desire, then I had to hate everything about myself that boys liked—my shyness, my sweetness, my beauty, my body. Feminism was about being a strong woman, so I hated myself for not being strong. It was about being assertive, so I hated myself for not being more assertive. It was about taking self-defense classes and fighting back, so I hated myself for not fighting back.

This is my dirtiest little secret: deep down, I have always believed I was not raped enough to call myself a survivor.

It is a horrible thing to say, something I would never, ever say to someone else. But somehow I came to believe that I do not deserve the same compassion as everyone else. Somehow I am at fault in a way no one else could ever be.

This is one of so many shames that are too common for trauma survivors: my experience wasn't bad enough. I did not earn the right to this suffering. I made it up. In some twisted way, I must have chosen it. It must be my fault.

If you've read my novel *Beautiful*, you know a little about the year I turned thirteen. It is the story of a girl not being in control of her own life, of being taken advantage of by everyone around her. It is the story of a girl falling, with no one to catch her, with no parents paying attention, no one protecting her, no one guarding her from so many experiences she was not ready for. It is a story of powerlessness. It is a story of desperation, of a kid who just needs someone to see her, someone to care, who needs an adult to step in and protect her. It is a story about grown-ups not doing their job.

It is a year that I am still sometimes amazed I survived. At a new school in a new town, I fell under the seduction of a manipulative and emotionally abusive girl who essentially acted as a pimp for my junior high's ninth-grade boys, trading access to my body in order to increase her own social standing. Some part of me felt strangely grateful for this—as objectifying as it was, it made me valuable. My body, the fact that it was wanted, gave me worth. So I did not question it when, only a few weeks into seventh grade, she delivered me, high on strong drugs I had never even heard of before that night, to the boy who wanted me the most, the highest bidder in terms of social currency. I did not question being in his bed. I did not question what we were doing. I would have done anything, but we were interrupted and I had a curfew. Another girl came after me that night and gave him what he wanted, and he no longer wanted me. I had failed. I had lost my worth.

I learned that giving boys what they wanted made me valuable, so that's what I did from then on. That friend soon turned on me for reasons I still don't fully understand and bullied me so severely that my parents had to call the police and I had to change schools. I felt more worthless than ever, but being wanted by boys at the new school gave me worth. I never even considered saying no. I never even considered thinking about what *I* wanted. Shortly after starting the new school, I became the girlfriend of the ninth-grade boy who was most persistent. I did whatever he wanted. I closed my eyes and learned how to make myself numb. I discovered the switch inside me that would turn my feelings off. I got high. I fell into drug addiction easily, as if it were made for me. I did whatever I could to make it not hurt. I learned how to die.

And again. And then again. And maybe some of the guys even had real feelings for me. Maybe it was possible for me to have had feelings for them. That boyfriend I had in seventh grade said he loved me and I said I loved him back, but I was lying. As soon as I gave him my body, he turned into something dead. I was dead. Any possibility of a real relationship was dead. He joined the great cemetery of all the dead guys.

In retrospect, I do not think these boys knew how much they were hurting me. Maybe they would have stopped if I had said no. Maybe they wouldn't have. I will never know. These are not useful questions, but I keep asking them. These questions are part of the abuse I heap onto myself: How much was my fault?

Is it ever the fault of a thirteen-year-old when she has sex that wounds her to her core?

That thirteen-year-old version of myself still lives inside me. She whispers on repeat: *You should have said no. You should have said no.* Her voice is cruel, hateful. She would never say this to anyone but me.

I remember going to the school nurse in high school, seeing a poster on the wall explaining the different degrees of statutory rape:

> *Rape of a child in the third degree: Child is at least 14, but less than 16 years old. Perpetrator is at least 48 months older than victim.*
> *Rape of a child in the second degree: Child is at least 12, but less than 14 years old. Perpetrator is at least 36 months older than the victim.*

I thought of the boys that could have fallen into these categories. Did they qualify? Were their ages off by a few months? I tried to picture them in jail. It did not seem right. I hated them, but I did not think they were rapists. They were kids too. Older than me, yes. But still kids.

But I remember feeling a glimmer of something inside, something like being seen, like maybe I did have some validation of my pain, that maybe my story was enough to earn the brokenness I felt, that maybe all those women marching against rape were marching for me, too. But that feeling did not last long. I convinced myself it was a stupid poster. Those were stupid rules made by stupid adults who had no idea what was really going on. How could they call something rape that was not rape? How could it be rape if I never said no, if the person who did it was a kid too?

All I know is I was barely thirteen years old when I lost my virginity. I was a child. I was not ready to consent to anything.

Laws will never be able to explain the feeling of a girl's soul dying.

I spent the summer between my freshman and sophomore years of college in South America, much of it in a little mountain village in Ecuador with my friend who had been living there for a year already. By then my drug addiction and alcoholism had firmly established itself, and my mental illness was not properly medicated. I spent those months in and out of various states of inebriation and emotional extremes.

One night, a guy in our general social circle, a foot taller and at least ten years older than me, followed me home from the bar.

I did not like him. He was annoying and talked all the time and never bathed. But he seemed harmless. He was the guy the other guys made fun of.

By that point I had already fended off a couple of old truckers who knocked on my motel room door one night, bottles of liquor in their hands, asking if I wanted to party. I had a reputation around town. I was the American girl who never said no.

But I did say no that night. I said it many times. I said it with my voice, in many different ways, in Spanish and in English, as he stood outside my door with his goofy grin trying to convince me to let him in. I said it with my body after he got tired of words, as he pushed on my door and I pushed back, as he lodged his foot in the doorway so it couldn't close. And the whole time, both of us smiling, because he was the friendly hippie and I was so goddamned *nice*, and it was just a game, a silly little game between friends, and we were both in on the joke. Even though he sickened me, even though I was scared, even though I meant every single no I said. It was not a joke to me at all.

After so many years of silence, I finally said no. But it didn't matter. He didn't believe me. After all, I had a reputation. I had slept with that married guy a few nights before. I was drunk. I'd dance with anyone at the club. All a girl like me needs is a little persuasion.

So I stopped saying no. I got tired. I felt the weight of inevitability: he was not going to take no for an answer. I could fight or I could get it over with. I knew how to get it over with. I had been doing that for years.

By the time I emerged from my room the next morning, hung over and wanting to die, the news had already spread around the village. My friend laughed and said, "I can't believe you slept with him. You *hate* him." Like it was a big joke, like I had chosen to do something funny. Yes, I hated him. But now I hated myself more.

These boys and men are ghosts. None of them have edges. They bleed into one another. They are the same. The only thing real is the thirteen-year-old girl underneath them, the girl who still lives inside me, the girl who shows herself whenever I am scared, who lends me her armor, her closed-off heart, even when I do not want her to. Sometimes it is this girl who still runs things.

The boys are part of a machine. Maybe each of them, individually, are not bad people. But something in the cumulative effect of them, something about being the girl I was in the body I had—something was taken. My choice was stolen, not by one physical act of assault, but by a combination of powers outside my control—my young age, my lack of education around sexuality, my emotionally unavailable parents, the trauma of transition and living in what I perceived to be an unsafe environment, my emotionally abusive friend, a culture of masculinity that does not teach boys to question silence and does not train them to know what it looks like when a girl's lights go out. Even the guy in Ecuador probably had no idea what was going on inside me. He was probably taught, like so many guys, that sometimes girls play hard to get, that sometimes they just need a little persuasion, that sometimes no really means yes. He probably had no idea that coercion is part of sexual assault. He probably thought I consented. He has no idea that he raped me.

I used to be angry at them, but now my anger is more nebulous. These boys are a symptom of a much bigger problem, of a society that does not teach its boys to truly understand what consent is. The boys of my youth did not know they were doing anything wrong. They were young and horny and grateful that they had what they thought was a willing participant. They did not know the extent of the damage they were causing.

I forgive those boys now, so many years later. But I do not forgive the society that created them. I do not forgive the society that created Brock Turner and Donald Trump, that lets men like them get away with hurting women, hurting an entire nation. I do not forgive a culture where masculinity is defined by conquest. I do not forgive the culture that forces girls to have to defend themselves, that shames us when we can't. I do not forgive the misogyny that turns women against one another, that makes us judge other women for not being woman enough, that makes us judge and hate ourselves.

Rape culture is the culture of silence. It's the culture of girls thinking a boy's desires trumps their own. It's the culture of girls thinking they're choiceless, of girls thinking their bodies are the most valuable parts of themselves and their worth is determined by how much they are wanted. It's slut shaming and victim blaming. It's parents not talking openly with their children about consent. It's parents not talking to girls about their entitlement to pleasure. It's parents not talking to their children about sex at all.

I have been publishing young adult fiction for ten years now. I have been writing different versions of that girl who lives inside me—the lost girl, the scared girl, the girl tearing herself apart. But some things happened in the last few years that started to change my writing. That started to change me. That started to change my feminism.

More than anything, it was the birth of my daughter that turned me radical. There is something about being a mother that has awakened my desire to save the world. I no longer have the privilege of not caring what happens to it. Because my heart is now outside my body. My heart is in the wild. She walks around in the world, vulnerable. My instinct is to defend her fiercely, to do everything I can to make the world safe for her, to make it safe for all the little girls like her.

I am blessed to work among the most passionate and compassionate people I have ever known—young adult authors. Our community is fierce in our love for our readers, and we feel a deep responsibility to them, especially teen girls. Our readers are our hearts in the wild. They are the girls still inside us, desperate to be seen and heard and loved. Our books are acts of love.

Two recent novels in particular moved me to my core—*All the Rage* by Courtney Summers, and *The Way I Used to Be* by Amber Smith. Courtney's book is about a girl who is raped and tells, but who is met with hostility and rejection by her entire community. Amber's book is about a girl who is raped but doesn't tell, who lets the secret destroy her from the inside. In both stories, the girl was alone. She had to survive what happened alone.

I was alone.

I wrote my novel *The Nowhere Girls* partly in response to these brilliant books. The characters haunted me. I felt a mix of anger and love, a mother's desire to protect them and lash out at those who hurt them. Not just them, but that thirteen-year-old girl still inside me. Not just her, but all the girls. Myself. My readers. My daughter.

I wanted to write a book about what could happen if those girls didn't have to be alone. What if they had been supported? What if they had been believed? What would happen if girls organized to take care of one another? What if girls unified to resist the culture that makes rape possible? What if we were *all* in this together? What would our power look like? What could we accomplish?

It's only now, writing this essay, that I realize I was writing *The Nowhere Girls* for myself. For that girl inside me who, at age thirteen, felt irreparably broken; who, at age sixteen, so desperately wanted a women's march against rape to include her, too;

who, at age nineteen, needed a friend's compassion, not ridicule.

I wrote a community for the girl alone inside me. I wrote best friends who believed her. I wrote her a whole army of girls to defend and protect her. I wrote her a path to healing.

Maybe sometimes I don't know how to fight for myself. But I will always fight for my readers, I will always fight for my daughter, and, in that fight, in those bold acts of unconditional love, maybe I will keep learning how to turn some of it back on the girl inside me who, these days, is feeling a little less lonely. Maybe it will get easier. Maybe we will keep working together to show one another how to love just a little bit better.

This is my feminism.

UNEXPECTED PURSUITS: EMBRACING MY INDIGENEITY & CREATIVITY

Christine Day

This essay was selected from the editor's call for submissions from unpublished writers.

When I think about my high school years, I often think about boxes.

I remember the squat, boxy buildings that comprised the campus. I remember the worn, institutional feel of the faded red bricks. I remember the rectangular classrooms, the perforated ceiling tiles, the bland white walls. I remember laminated library books, the gleaming expanse of the gymnasium, the sleek metal lockers that lined the halls.

I remember standardized tests, the information they requested, the boxes I checked: female; American Indian/Alaska Native (sometimes mixed-race/multiracial/other, if they had it); English, first language; US Citizen.

I remember career aptitude advisements, college planning sheets, interest assessments.

I look back at all those plans and am relieved to share: I didn't follow any of it.

In retrospect, it's difficult to describe how I felt as a high school student. As someone who spent her adolescence in that rigid space, growing and changing and breathing but doing so almost invisibly. I was always a little apprehensive of my surroundings. Something about the school made me feel claustrophobic. The classes I took often left me uneasy. Looking back now, I realize these feelings probably stemmed from my Indigenous identity, my personal history.

I should begin by saying that I wasn't raised on a reservation. I grew up in a suburb just outside of Seattle, Washington, and attended a school with an approximate 0.5 percent Native American population. Our campus was built in occupied Duwamish lands, but I don't recall anyone ever mentioning this.

I attended history classes in which Indigenous perspectives were almost entirely erased. Their civilizations, their treaties, their resilience, their agency: all absent from the textbooks, gone without a trace. I attended science classes, which were entrenched in biology, ecology, and environmental activism, without integrating Indigenous values or knowledge systems. I wrote countless essays in my English classes, and yet I don't remember any Indigenous-centered prompts or research options.

I memorized SAT vocabulary words despite how useless they were in everyday communication. (Meanwhile, letters from the Nooksack Tribe—where my mother is enrolled—arrived at our house, advertising programs for language revitalization.)

We were the thunderbirds. I remember our crest: a lightning bolt pierced the school's green initials, sealed inside a royal blue shield. A banner with our full name unfurled beneath it, and two nondescript evergreen trees stood alongside it. Our mascot was perched at the top, gray wings spread wide, motionless.

In traditional stories and oral histories, Thunderbird holds significance and power. In my high school, this iconic figure became a frozen caricature. A stenciled silhouette, deprived of movement and color.

I took a career aptitude test in my sophomore year. It was a class assignment, something I did to get full credit. When the results came back, I penciled in my post–high school plan:

The test claimed I would be a good nurse. I wrote the job title down, imagined how my life would turn out, and decided I liked it. I could live with it. Nurses were important; the world could always use more of them. Plus, I could finish my education after spending two years at a community college.

That was good; I found it reassuring.

I submitted the assignment, and tried to forget about it.

* * *

Throughout high school, my grades remained average at best. Teachers wrote lukewarm comments in my progress reports: *Is a pleasure to have in class, but could put forth more effort. Is well-mannered and cooperative, but has several missing assignments. Demonstrates a need for consistent motivation. Expresses ideas clearly in writing.*

They thought I was bright, but they also thought I was a problem. I could feel it when they returned my assignments, papers delicately folded to hide their red ink scribbles. I could hear it in their sighs, each time I "forgot my homework at my house."

There were some exceptions. I remember my US Government & History teacher, my junior year. She took an interest in me and regularly checked in to see how I was doing. She also veered from the typical curriculum, delving into topics other teachers avoided for the sake of "neutrality" and "political correctness." She taught us to look for biases across different news outlets. She showed us graphic images from wars and protests. She directed our attention away from the textbooks, where history was presented in a sterile, linear version of events. And she introduced us to other renditions that were grittier, darker, more volatile.

She still had rules to follow. Limitations to work around. But her class was one of the first that really mattered to me. I realized there were real stakes in the decisions I made. I realized that history unfolds based on the work that happens in the present.

I also created my first documentary film in her class.

The assignment adhered to the National History Day prompt, "Innovation in History: Impact and Change." My ten-minute film was about Lewis Hine, the photographer who helped reform child labor laws in America. I submitted it to the National History Day competition, where it was selected as a regional finalist. My teacher gave me an A and asked for a DVD copy of the documentary. She wanted to use it in her curriculum for future classes.

Lewis Hine was one of the first activists to ever wield a camera. He photographed children in factories, coal mines, seafood canneries. He learned the names of newspaper boys, noted the heights of farm workers, recorded the wages earned in mills. He snuck into these industrial complexes, sometimes posing as a fire inspector, a postcard vendor, a Bible salesman. He risked threats of violence and legal action, but that never stopped him from documenting these realities of injustice. He recognized the wrongness, and he did something about it.

He helped change the course of history.

Toward the end of my senior year, I was summoned to a small room on campus for a video interview. Some of my classmates were working on a DVD that would be distributed to our graduating class, a memento we could keep tucked inside our yearbooks.

The interview was short, straightforward.

I told them my name was Christine Day. After graduation I

was going to attend community college and pursue a degree in nursing.

Not long afterward, I remember this exchange I had with my partner:

Mazen and I were at his house, seated in the kitchen, sharing a plate of hummus and labneh drizzled in olive oil. In between bites, I told him about how excited I was to graduate, to start working toward my two-year degree in nursing.

Mazen broke off a piece of pita bread and then paused.

Something about his posture, his body language, made me ask, "What?"

He looked at me and said, "Is that really what you want?"

"Um. Yes?" For some reason, his question confused me.

He just kept staring. And I had this sense that he saw something I couldn't see.

I asked him, "Why are you looking at me like that?"

And he said, "What about your writing?"

My final graduation requirement was simple.

I had to prepare a capstone presentation of my best work and achievements. And once again I had to announce my future career path, my plans post-graduation.

I had a binder filled with relevant artifacts and information. The original test results were there, saved from my sophomore year. My career plan, detailed passionlessly in my lazy handwriting, was tucked between all these other files: essays, poetry, short stories, reflections on other creative projects, like the Lewis Hine documentary.

The creative writing. The documentary. They kept resurfacing. They kept coming back to me.

As a high school freshman I took a class called World History & Geography. It was taught by a well-meaning white man, who often held his coffee thermos like a goblet and paced around the room, announcing due dates like a stage actor performing a monologue. He used his class time to introduce us to various, fascinating regions. I don't remember much from the course as a whole, aside from concise little snippets: a PowerPoint presentation with photographs of Machu Picchu, which my teacher dreamily described as a destination he'd love to go to; pop quizzes focused on religions practiced across the Middle East and Asia; blank maps of the African continent, which we were tasked to fill in.

One day, I remember my teacher mentioning something about the Nez Perce Indians. I don't remember the full context of the lesson. I couldn't say for sure if he addressed them in the past or present tense. I don't remember anything about it, except for this: when he pronounced their name, he said, "Nay Pierce."

Now, I was only fifteen years old at the time, and extremely shy. But the moment I heard him say this, I felt my cheeks burn bright red, while my bones turned to ice.

He wasn't saying it right. I knew he wasn't, because of what my mother had told me about my heritage. My maternal grandmother was Upper Skagit/Nooksack, a Coast Salish woman, indigenous to what is now northwestern Washington, and southwestern Canada. My maternal grandfather was Blackfeet/Nez Perce, a Plateau man, indigenous to what is now eastern Washington, Idaho, and Montana.

Before I could stop myself, my hand shot up, and I cut off his lecture. "That's not how you pronounce it."

There was a brief, uncomfortable silence. I don't think I had ever interrupted a teacher like that in my life. And I'd clearly caught him off guard; he looked almost alarmed by the sound of my voice.

"It's Nez Perce. That's how they say it."

"Hm. I don't think so." He frowned a little, clearly confused by my outburst. "The name Nez Perce was given to them by the French. It means 'pierced nose.' And to my understanding, those two words are pronounced 'Nay Pierce.'"

My palms were slick with sweat. My heart thudded hesitantly inside my rib cage.

"I'm a descendant," I said. "My mother is full Native American." For some reason, I felt compelled to add this, the fullness of her blood quantum. "She comes from four tribes, including the Nez Perce."

Again, I remember a silence. This awkward shift in the room's power dynamics.

In their own Sahaptin language, the Nez Perce call themselves the *Nimíipuu*, which translates to "The People."

* * *

The senior capstone presentations were scheduled in random locations on campus. Mine was assigned to the same classroom my World History & Geography class had been in.

I walked in, dressed in black slacks and a silk button-down shirt, my binder tucked under my arm. My parents, sister, and partner were all there. And so were a handful of other seniors, along with their own parents and supporters. Plus, the capstone supervisor, my former video production teacher.

As the presentations began, I thought about my time in high school, how I spent it. I reflected on the choices I made, the ones that felt right, the ones that didn't. I thought about the times I spoke up, and the times I shouldn't have remained silent. I thought about the paper with my two-year nursing plan, the speech I'd prepared on my notecards, and this space I was sitting in. And I reached for that safe, content feeling I had, when I claimed I wanted to become a nurse.

But it wouldn't come. That feeling no longer existed.

Maybe it never had.

And when my turn came, I thought: *Screw it. Here goes nothing.*

I cleared my throat and began my presentation.

I told them my name was Christine Day. After graduation, I was going to attend community college and then probably transfer to a four-year university. I was interested in creative writing and would like to write books one day.

* * *

I got my first tattoo that summer. I walked into the boutique parlor, introduced myself to the smiling artist, and showed her my lavender dream catcher.

The dream catcher was a gift my parents had given me when I was a toddler. It had hung in my room all throughout my childhood years. At this point in my life I didn't think of dream catchers as appropriated objects. All I knew was that this particular one was symbolic of my home, my background, my adolescence. There were things about the early chapters of my life that I never wanted to forget.

So I paid the artist to create a drawing of it, which became a stencil she pressed against my back, which she then inked into my skin.

I spent two years in community college. They were wonderful. I loved it.

I cherished the freedom that came with selecting my classes, many of which were challenging in content. My grades improved drastically from my high school years, and I started to feel more comfortable and capable as a student.

I took plenty of writing and literature classes. I immersed myself in the humanities. I drafted short stories and chapters for projects I imagined could be novel-length someday. I spent hours alone with my thoughts, dreaming up metaphors, spinning characters and plots.

* * *

Mazen and I were in his car, passing through some residential neighborhood. I remember the opaqueness of the zinc-colored sky. I remember the rhythm of the windshield wipers, the teary streaks that smeared across the windowpane. The billowing warmth of the heat vents; the closeness of our car seats. I watched his profile as he drove, admiring the concentration on his handsome face.

And then, out of nowhere, I said, "I'm gonna do it."

He glanced at me, one brow arched, curious. "You're gonna do what?"

"Write. I'm gonna do it. I've been researching the publishing process lately, and I'm not going to wait until I finish school. I'm just going to start trying now. And I'll keep trying, no matter how long it takes."

Mazen smirked. He looked out at the road ahead and placed his hand on my knee. "Yeah," he said. "You are."

From that declaration onward, I started writing all kinds of drafts.

My first full manuscript was written over the course of two years. It was some odd variation of a dystopian young adult novel, which was what I'd mainly been reading around that time. And it was horrible.

My second attempt was a supernatural, contemporary retelling of *Wuthering Heights*. Or at least, I pitched it as such, despite it being an extremely loose interpretation. And it was awful.

My third attempt was about a teenage girl whose mother

hires a paranormal reality TV crew to investigate their house for ghosts. And it was garbage. An actual, steaming pile.

My fourth attempt—I haven't given up on that one; I don't think I ever will.

In addition to my (many, rejected) manuscripts, I drafted other things, too.

I produced more essays and stories in my community college classes.

And when the time came, I wrote statements for my university application.

Spoiler alert: I was accepted.

My next two tattoos were swallows.

I returned to the same artist and explained to her what I wanted. I asked her to borrow some of the colors she'd used in my dream catcher, to use them in dapples and shades across their bodies. Other than that, I didn't have any formal requests. I gave her artistic license to fill in the colors as she liked, to make the birds beautiful and bold and bright.

She drew the outline and created two stencils that were mirror images of the same swallow. She positioned them over my shoulder blades, high enough for the tips of the wings and tails to curl over my shoulders. The birds looked like they were soaring inward, their beaks pointed toward my dream catcher.

Swallows are popular among tattoo enthusiasts because

these tiny birds always know how to return home. No matter how far they go, they have this uncanny ability to find their way back.

I transferred to the University of Washington–Bothell. I declared Culture, Literature, and the Arts as my major.

I attended a wide range of classes. Most were random, spontaneous. I was exposed to research interests I'd never considered, things I wouldn't have associated with academics. My horizons were broadened in the realms of literature and art, history and science and society, writing and expression and creativity. These classes opened up whole new vocabularies, alternative ways of reading and experiencing.

I vividly remember the moment I learned the word "diaspora." It was something I was intimately familiar with, though I had no idea it could be encapsulated in the English language.

When my professor shared it in class, I penned the definition furiously into my notes, my hand cramping as I left indents in the paper. *The movement, migration, or scattering of a people from an established homeland; the people so dispersed, often by force.* In that moment, I felt completely, truly reflected in my education.

I thought about my mother's adoption. I thought about how I lived in the Pacific Northwest, the Coast Salish region, my own ancestral homelands. I thought about my deep love for this landscape, as well as the simultaneous, paradoxical disconnect from it I'd inherited.

"Diaspora." It conjured a sharp-edged feeling. It plucked at something raw inside me.

As my undergraduate career came to a swift end, I started to panic. More than anything, I still wanted to write books, but despite how many I created, how many I submitted, nothing was sticking. It wasn't working. And in the midst of all those rejections, college was ending. But I still had so many unanswered questions. I was lost, adrift in a current I couldn't counteract, all over again.

I found the program almost by accident.

I'd been contemplating grad school for some time, debating the merits of an MFA in creative writing, or the possibility of pursuing a master's in library science. I wasn't sure how I'd pay for additional schooling. I wasn't sure which path I wanted to take, now that I found myself at a new crossroads. I just knew I wanted to keep going.

And then I came across it. A master's program called Native Voices, located at the University of Washington.

Native Voices is a documentary filmmaking program, with an Indigenous emphasis. Students are encouraged to engage with cultural, personal, and social issues in their own lives. To research, create, and collaborate in partnership with Indigenous communities.

I couldn't believe it. It was perfect.

* * *

In the midst of another tattoo session, I told my artist about my new plan. She knew I was about to graduate from UW Bothell, and when I told her about Native Voices, she was impressed, but also a little skeptical.

"You know, you might be able to create a film like that without having to go to school. Just buy some equipment, submit your work to film festivals, do it all on your own. It would probably save you a ton of money. Stuff like that is so accessible now."

I understand why she thought that. But as she filled in my red-violet camellia blossoms, I couldn't help but interject.

I told her about my mother's adoption. Prior to the Indian Child Welfare Act of 1978, about one-third of Native children were removed from their families. She was among them. Her relationships with her parents and community were severed the day she was born. This was all part of the Baby Scoop Era, as well as the US Government's cultural genocide against Natives. I told my tattoo artist about this chapter of American history, which I never learned about in school but lived with every day. I told her I still had a lot to learn. That I wanted to remember these colonial disruptions, but I also wanted to move forward toward cultural revitalization. That I wanted to mend these relationships, return to these communities, and serve them. I told her that was why I'd come to her in the first place, with my dream catcher and those two swallows. They were more than just tattoos. They represented a promise I intended to keep, an oath I'd forged into my skin.

By the time I was done, she nodded. She understood.

* * *

I spent weeks on my Native Voices application.

I called their information number, to clarify questions I had about the process. I drafted multiple versions of my résumé, my personal statement. I pulled almost everything I had, in hopes that it would work out. I told them I'd made it onto the University of Washington's Annual Dean's List. I wrote about my desire to connect with and contribute to Indigenous communities. I wrote about the importance of reclaiming film, of transforming it into a medium of healing. I wrote about the political power and history behind this practice and how I'd familiarized myself with it when I created a documentary on Lewis Hine as a high school student.

I gave it everything. And within a few short months I received notice that I was in.

A few weeks later I walked at the UW Bothell graduation.

I wore my black ceremony robe. I decorated my cap to look like a purple-and-gold clapperboard, advertising the fact that I was bound for grad school, a soon-to-be student in Native Voices. Before the ceremony started, my parents bought me a lei of flowers and my sister gifted me a necklace laced with candy bars.

I left the stadium with my robe unzipped, my graduation cap tucked under one arm. The fragrant flowers and crinkly candy bars were cool against my skin. My curls were long and loose, deflating from the heat and humidity. My heels tapped against the sidewalk in a brisk, clipped beat.

Mazen called me. He was looking for me. I tried to describe where I was, but the parking lots were expansive and confusing. I spun around and around, searching for him, explaining everything I could see.

Finally, I found him. He was coming down the same sidewalk, from the opposite end of the lot. He had a bouquet of red roses and a huge smile, sunshine glancing off his sunglasses. I beamed and ran toward him. And as the gap closed between us, I was certain of every step, confident in the direction I was going.

When I think about Native Voices, I often think about connections.

I think about our classes, our discussions, our reassurances, our solidarity. I think about my professors, who have supported me in stressful moments and been patient as I grappled with my research interests. I think about Indigenous events on campus, in which the Duwamish people are always acknowledged. I think about the people I've met and am grateful for their laughter, their survival, their wisdom. I think about Indigenous identity as a living, changing practice. I think about decolonization as the real definition of progress, and I think about how it looks as an ongoing process.

I think about how I fit into these communities, this world, these times I'm living in.

I think about my responsibilities as an artist, a scholar, an Indigenous woman.

* * *

My name is Christine Day. I'm descendant from four Indigenous nations and an enrolled member of the Upper Skagit. I'm a graduate student, working toward my master's degree in Indigenous Research and Documentary Film Production. I'm currently filming interviews to accompany my film, my future thesis. And I'm also working on projects in prose. I still haven't given up on those.

I'm a work in progress. I'm young, and I'm growing; I always have been. And it's taken me a long time to understand this. But listen: You are never alone in these in-between places. Your thoughts, your complex feelings, your unknowable questions—they mean something, and they're important.

Never dismiss your own perspectives. Never question the validity of life in the margins.

CHILLED MONKEY BRAINS

Sona Charaipotra

"Chilled monkey brains."

Those three words—casually uttered during a particularly racist scene from the eighties classic movie *Indiana Jones and the Temple of Doom*—haunted me for much of my childhood, long into teendom, and now even as an adult.

The pain they caused seared fresh flesh recently as I stumbled upon the film while flipping channels (it's a thing we used to do before Netflix and Hulu) with my daughter, who's seven. She was enthralled at first by the action and adventure, and the fact that it was a rare instance of seeing brown people—like her and me—reflected on the screen. But as Harrison Ford and his oh-so-blond love interest sat down to share a meal with the very brown keepers of the Raj, something went terribly awry. The lavish spread included insects and roaches, some steaming, some still crawling off the plate (and right down the terrified blond lady's dress, of course). And for dessert? You guessed it: "chilled monkey brains."

"But we don't eat that, Mama!" Kavya declared with disgust. "Why would they say that?"

Why indeed? But racist images like these—and the bobble-headed Apu of *The Simpsons* Kwik-E-Mart fame—were the only images of myself I saw on-screen as a kid in the nineties. Perhaps just as relevant, they were the only images other kids in my small town saw of brown people too. And naturally, they stuck.

I was four when we moved to the United States. Growing up in suburban New Jersey, I was the only Indian kid in my class, my kid sister the only one in hers. Dorky, bookish, and brown, complete with braces and glasses, I stood out among my peers. I tried to blend in, to hide in the back of the class, not raising my hand, preferring to bury my nose in a book, living among fictional friends like Jo March of *Little Women* and Anne Shirley of *Anne of Green Gables*. Not realizing back then that even in those pages where I found solace, *I* was nowhere to be seen.

In school, though, as much as I tried to be invisible, I couldn't help but get noticed.

"If I come over, can we have some chilled monkey brains?" I got asked in school on several occasions. "Or maybe roasted roaches?"

I learned hard and fast not to bring traditional Indian food—like my mom's delicious potato-stuffed paranthas or spicy thari chicken and rice—to school for lunch. "That stinks" was the usual reaction. My classmates saw a pale, sickly version of a certain horrific mealtime scene from an outrageously racist movie—one in which I was always cast as the bad guy. And I took it to heart, opting instead for stale, boring—and safe—peanut butter sandwiches every single day. And coming to school with post-celebration mehendi—the intricate, meaningful swirl of henna inking my skin—on my hands was asking for trouble too. The other kids didn't see the beauty in it. Instead they'd mock it as scary or gross, making me question the majesty of centuries of tradition.

But really, those were microaggressions. The big picture—I learned as I grew—was even more dangerous. I remember in middle school, the fury of lockers slammed with the force of anger—a kid livid at *me* about Saddam Hussein, who had absolutely nothing to do with me (except that we both had brown skin). The kid was so obviously repeating what he heard at home, trying on his parents' adult-sized racism, displacing his aggression onto me. It was a real act of violence, and it reflected the state of central New Jersey in the late 1980s and early 1990s, when tensions simmered and a hate group called the Dotbusters—so called because of the bindi many married Indian women wear on their foreheads—terrorized whole towns. I was too young—and honestly, scared—to dig too deep into what was happening then. But now, many years later, I read about it and my blood runs cold: the first murder (along with most of the other violent attacks) the Dotbusters committed happened in the very town I now call home. Nearly sixty hate crimes were reported then—think about how many must have gone unreported.

Years later, my dad told me of the very real fears that haunted middle-class Desi immigrants. There were the intangible (but still obvious and painful consequences), like blatant racism and discrimination when it came to finding work and housing. But there were also more pointed and disturbing incidents—like the time my father found a flaming bag of shit (yes, for real) on our front porch in the middle of the night. As a family, we managed to muddle through as best we could, not ruffling feathers, contributing to the community, where my parents were pediatricians with their own practice after years of redoing residencies and rotations to meet American medical standards, facing a lot of racism along the way.

As kids, too, my siblings and I tried to blend, obsessing over teen idols like the New Kids on the Block and *NSYNC, singing in choirs (and alt-rock bands, in the case of my brother), going to dances where no one really asked us to dance. Visits to the temple faded fast in favor of the white plastic Christmas tree, bought in true Desi fashion at a garage sale, that we used for years, and the annual Diwali lights stayed up through New Year's, showing that we celebrated all the holidays.

In high school and college, pop culture was the thing I turned to when I was in search of community—the fandoms were a rare place where it didn't matter what you looked like or where you "really came from." I was a diehard "Blockhead," as the New Kids fans called themselves (my favorite then was sweet Joey, although I secretly had a thing for bad-boy Donnie, too!), and my sister and I wrote fan fiction to entertain ourselves and others. When I wasn't listening to mopey, broken-hearted ballads, I had my nose buried in a book, moving from my beloved *Anne of Green Gables* and the Baby-Sitters Club series to *The Vampire Diaries* and the YA classics by Judy Blume and her kin. Books were an indulgence my mother allowed, and I was lucky enough to have new ones to lose myself in every month. I even wrote short bits here and there, getting encouragement from occasional teachers who took note of the quiet shuffling in the back of the room. It wasn't until much later—in my college days—that I realized what I'd been missing even there, in my own work: a reflection of myself. The very first stories I wrote were full of white people. It was the world I lived in.

Later, I'd read short stories and novels by Indian authors like Kiran Desai and Chitra Banerjee Divakaruni. But in one book—then published as adult but perhaps now it would be categorized as YA—I finally found her, a girl like me. Not exactly, of course. She was Muslim to my pseudo-Hindu (a discussion for another day), from Boston, and far more troubled.

But the star of Ameena Meer's *Bombay Talkie* was a teenage brown girl of Indian descent, living in modern-day America. In her, I found my angst, my personal teen triumphs and traumas, echoed.

I got to meet the author when she came to do a signing at Rutgers, where I was studying journalism and American Studies, much to my parents' chagrin. I told Ameena how my parents had begged me to be a doctor like them, to one day take over their practice. But I was thinking, maybe, just maybe, I could be a writer, too. With her encouragement, I signed up for a screenwriting class in my senior year, and I've been actively writing ever since, interning at magazines and landing my (then) dream job as a reporter at *People* magazine, where I got to interview idols like the former New Kids (Joey McIntyre chews his cuticles—just thought you should know) and the author Jhumpa Lahiri, whose short stories had me smitten.

After the events of September 11, though, things took a dark turn. I was in New York City that day, working at *People*, writing a story on the Video Music Awards back when they were relevant, having spent the weekend covering Beyoncé's birthday party (yes, really). My dad called me first thing that Tuesday morning, as I was walking to work, and said these words: "The Twin Towers are no more." Like they were people who had died. And, of course, they *were* people who had died—some three thousand people, with names and faces and stories we'd spend the next several news cycles unraveling. I was one of the few reporters who showed up at *People* that day, and in between interviewing strangers who were already mourning loved ones lost, I bawled constantly. That day fundamentally changed how I saw myself as a person. Time and again I'd been told I was the fluffy girl. That my interests in books and movies and pop culture were lacking depth and meaning, even as I wrote academic papers analyzing Madonna's place in the feminist canon and how boy bands created a safe space for teen girls to explore their sexuality. Now I was covering the major story of our lifetime—albeit through tears. I was stronger than I thought—and in the days and months and years after 9/11, I learned I'd have to find and raise my voice.

But that tragic moment fundamentally changed the way my fellow Americans viewed me and the other brown bodies among us. Just four days later, the first murder happened. Balbir Singh Sodhi, a Sikh-American man, was gunned down in a hate crime in Mesa, Arizona. When I pitched that story to my editors, it was rejected—because there was no way to make the ending more upbeat. The hate crimes haven't stopped since. Avtar Singh, murdered in 2003. The six lives lost at the Oak Creek gurdwara in Wisconsin in 2012. Prabhjot Singh, beaten unconscious in Central Park, yes, in my New York City, in 2015.

The anti-immigrant, anti-Muslim, anti-LGBTQIA, anti-anti-anti sentiment of Trump's America—not my America—has given new fuel to this already raging fire. Within the few days of writing this essay, countless brown people have faced violent acts of domestic terrorism—because let's call it what it is—at the hands of white nationalists. By the time this goes to press, four of them are dead. Who knows how many others there will be. Because of the ever-escalating rhetoric of hate against anyone who is non-white, non-hetero, non-cis, non-Christian, and so on, these hate crimes will continue to happen. In fact, in the ten days after the 2016 election, nearly nine hundred hate incidents were reported to the Southern Poverty Law Center. That's about ninety a day. The SPLC also reports that the growth of active hate groups has increased for the second consecutive year as Trump continues to electrify the radical right. And this hate profoundly impacts children. In a post-election survey of ten thousand educators, 90 percent said the climate at their schools had been negatively affected by the campaign. Eighty percent described heightened anxiety and fear among students, particularly immigrants, Muslims, and African-Americans. And according to the Sikh Coalition, as of 2016, nearly 70 percent of turbaned Sikh children have been bullied in school. No doubt that number has since grown.

And recently, we've all seen the videos of kids—*kids*—telling their fellow students to go back to Mexico or Pakistan or Syria, calling them terrorists. We've seen brown people—many US citizens—detained at airports and deported to countries they haven't seen for years, even decades. We've seen the acts of violence and now the murders.

What does that have to do with "chilled monkey brains"? Only everything. The images we continue to perpetuate of certain people as *other* are exactly what leads to this kind of toxic environment. And it isn't always so horrific as the aforementioned "chilled monkey brains," but even the deceptively mild forms of racism on-screen and in pages are, when repeated unabated over time, profoundly sinister. Our cultures are constantly appropriated, the meaning of rich, relevant elements of our lives, cultures, religion, mythology, and rituals whitewashed (and frequently monetized) for mass consumption, stripping them of their history and context. It's in the constant, blatant, and accepted mispronunciation of "foreign" names (even for people born and raised in the United States), the endless and pointed "where are you really froms," the mocking bobblehead movements, or the thick, curry-coated accent. It's "you barely have an accent" when my only accent is Jersey. It's the casual (Coachella) cooption of bindis and mehndi and yoga when we were once teased for embracing these elements of our own culture. It's Bobby Flay on the Food Network attributing the popularity of "chai tea" (chai *is* tea, people) in the United States to a white woman from Oregon. It's Kali transformed into the effed-up villain of a schlocky horror flick without context, or Shiva dancing on a hippie-chic white woman's bag or T-shirt. It's Matt Damon saving China, and Scarlett and Emma playing Asian characters. It's publishers willing to put out a POC story, but only if it fits the white gaze narrative—like the model minority, the exotic seductress, the thug, or the happy slave. After all, oppression sells, right?

It's every time my story gets taken away from me, stripped of meaning and whitewashed for mass (read: white) consumption, telling me the version I want to tell is not relatable or real. It's the fact that these appropriated versions of our stories, decontextualized and whitewashed, hit the bestseller lists and make bank at the box office. It's debilitating and infuriating.

But things are shifting. #OwnVoices are rising up, reclaiming our stories and insisting on our own unvarnished truths. Movements like #WeNeedDiverseBooks, #OscarsSoWhite, and #YesAllWomen are creating a unified, resounding echo. Hopefully, publishers and producers are listening, and the kids of my daughter's generation—the ones who are hungrily looking for real representations of themselves on pages and screens right this moment—will not face the same othering or scarcity I and countless kids like me did growing up.

My kid will know that she—smart, resourceful, powerful, and brown—can be the hero of any story. In an ideal world, my kid—and other kids like her—will see herself reflected on-screen, in books, and in the media she consumes. She's excited to see shows like Disney's *Andi Mack*, with a half-Asian girl front and center in a *fun* story, or Priyanka Chopra starring on an ABC series (albeit as a potential terrorist). She loves Claudia Kishi—just like her mama did—because she's the Asian member of the Baby-Sitters Club, but also because she's the most fashionable one. And Ms. Marvel—brown and proud, from Jersey just like her—is my kid's role model. (She's even cosplayed her at Comic Con!)

But there's plenty more to be done. And it's up to us to do it. We have to raise our voices and create the change we want to see. Change comes slowly but surely, and there are smart, enthusiastic, determined women helming it in all arenas—but especially on-screen and on the page. I'm proud to be a part of that movement. As a writer and an entrepreneur, running the book packager CAKE Literary, I'm trying to make sure our stories are told—for us, by us. We create fun, delicious, un-put-downable books where the diversity is part of the story without becoming the whole story. Our diverse characters are so not the sidekicks. In *The Gauntlet*, a *Jumanji*-inspired action adventure, a hijabi girl is the hero. In *Love Sugar Magic*, a Mexican-American kid discovers the joys—and dangers—of playing with magic at her family's small-town Texas bakery. In my upcoming YA novel, an Indian teen from Jersey (not unlike me) is a girl genius doctor who works at the same hospital as her overbearing mom—and falls in love with a patient. These are American stories—and they look like real America today.

We all fight the best way we know how. And these days, for me, even as I weep during writing sprints at the ceaseless, terrible news that crashes like endless waves on a shore, I stumble through, knowing that the only power I may have is the words on the pages. And knowing, deep down, as a kid who was a reader and an adult who still believes in the power of words, that that's not nothing. Our voices are our power. We must use them—and teach the generations after us to do the same. Together, all those voices can create an epic boom. Maybe even one that can take down a wall.

ROAR

Jaye Robin Brown

Summer of fifteen. Baby fat disappeared. Curves tucked out and in just like the actresses on the big screen. Of course I had my own personal problem areas, but I reveled in my reflection. Somehow, after the breakouts cleared up and the training bra upgraded to an underwire, I'd started looking like the older girls I'd always admired and crushed on. I was woman. Hear me roar.

But it wasn't long before I discovered a problem with the roar. It brought unwanted attention. Roaring, to me, was about finding a place inside of myself where I was feeling like a grown-ass woman. But to others, that roar wasn't about who I was, but how I looked.

My fifteen-year-old summer was when my father decided I could have two swimsuits instead of one. Such a minor memory.

A yearly trek to the bathing suit shop while on a family beach vacation. My first try-on of a real eensy-weensy bikini, stepping out of the dressing room and having loads of eyes on me, and my father saying to my mom, "Why don't you get her two suits this year instead of one?" It remains, a niggling memory, the moment when the man I loved more than any man in the world saw me not for the bright creative sparks shooting off inside my head, but for the pleasing composition of my physical form. A first blow. A first shrinking in of myself. I forgave him, of course, because like so many men, his was an unaware tic, something so ingrained he didn't even realize he was doing it.

But, as a girl, it didn't take long for me to figure out we are not considered our own. There's a certain privilege men, some women, and the media carry, the right they feel to cast their gaze upon us and judge us fit or unfit based on the culmination of our physical parts. I saw it in the recent presidential election. Where a man judged his incredibly smart, talented, and capable daughter on her physical appearance, as if that were the pinnacle of her success. Or, more realistically, the pinnacle of his success. This bothered me as a teen. It continues to bother me now.

Growing up was complicated. I was raised in Deep South Alabama, where gender roles remain stronger than other areas and there's a rigidity that follows this form. You look like that? Well, then, you act like this. Not to say all women in the South are quivering mice, far from it. My mother has a PhD in marketing from a time when women just didn't do that. Yet she still fixed my father his breakfast and supper every single day while he sat and read the paper. She would argue that she loved and loves doing this for him, and I'm sure that's true, but I also think there's a cultural norm at play. A level of expectation that is as subconscious as breathing.

My feminine complexity was deeper than simply wanting to look like a girl. Turned out I wanted to buck some sexuality roles, too. What I didn't know in my teen years, because I didn't know it was allowed or possible, was that I was a lesbian. I had no lesbian role models. My parents had no lesbian friends. The closest I got were the two sisters who owned the riding stables where I took lessons. They had a "friend" who lived on the farm with them. My mother decided I would switch stables around the time I hit puberty. I still wonder if this was because, at some level, she knew and feared for my "corruption."

There were close calls with self-discovery during my teen years. The younger neighbor girl who I built a fort with in the woods. As we lay on the pine straw and took turns tickling each other with the feathery fronds, I had the kind of breath-less (and groin) feeling other friends were having with boys. A sleepover with a schoolmate where we practiced kissing after dark and I didn't want it to stop. An older neighbor who wanted to show me her room and my stomach lurched with excitement, before my mother interrupted by calling me back home. Tiny moments of titillation and rapid breathing when I found a girl attractive. But how was it even possible? I looked like a girly-girl. I was the kind of girl who would be with a boy. The male gaze told me so.

It was in the way the construction workers who pulled up outside my school catcalled me, a teen girl in a school uniform. It was the boat owner at the marina where I worked, who put his hands on me during a tour of his boat and when I stepped away, his blithe "I thought you wanted it," simply because I was dressed in my everyday boat-washing uniform of shorts and bikini top. It was the fraternity boys on the beach at spring break with their white score cards, numbered 0–10, that they would flash at passing girls from their low beach chairs, absolutely self-righteous in their actions even when they left us humiliated. I still have a visceral reaction to this memory.

I spent so much of my late teens and early twenties confused. I dated more boys than I should have. Being objectified as a teen had left me feeling like hooking up was the way to prove I was someone. By using my femininity to prove how desirable I was, I could be the Southern belle, the popular girl, the daughter I thought my father wanted. Even if I was unhappy inside. Even if I felt lost. Even if I was so much more than the way I looked on the outside.

Besides, being queer was confusing. Even though the guys were leering and whistling and totally willing to get with me, the lesbians didn't notice me. At least not many. Because I didn't conform to those norms either.

And for a while I was okay with that. The girls I allowed

myself to date in college were more questioning than queer and the one girl who was truly ready to be my girlfriend scared the shit out of me. I wasn't ready to be out and she was. I preferred the girls who wouldn't challenge me. One early girlfriend even said to me, "Once we finish with our husbands and our families we can find each other and live on a goat farm." That made sense to me at the time, putting off my true desires for something more socially acceptable. Passing was super easy. Being queer was not something feminine, Southern girls did. My father would hate me. My mother would wonder where she'd gone wrong. So I thought I'd just fake it until I made it. If I could pretend for long enough, maybe I would somehow, magically, change.

With those early patterns stamped hard onto my psyche, I tried everything I could to make my square peg fit in that round slot. I could conform and proved it by finding a very nice guy with a very good job who loved going to hear bands as much as I did. I thought, maybe this is what marriage is? You find a nice guy who is your friend, and even though your heart doesn't go *boom, boom, boom,* you marry him, because he'll be a good provider and never abuse you or your future children.

How wrong I was. Because even in marriage it was still there. The same nagging voice inside my psyche that I was living a wrong life. My husband was a gym rat, obsessed with his own physical looks, and so I became obsessed with mine. Was I thin enough, coiffed enough, pretty enough? I stayed on guard and insecure every single day. I judged myself by male standards. I felt like my whole world revolved around how I looked instead of who I was. I was miserable.

So I went into counseling. All I knew was I was terribly unhappy and self-medicating in ways that weren't good for me long-term. I still couldn't name my gay. I'd married a boy. I had long hair. I liked to wear makeup—that meant I was straight, right? But what did it mean that I still thought about the girls I'd known and wondered if being married meant I could never be with another girl again? I wondered if I did, would it be cheating?

When I did finally fall hard in love, in a way that made not coming out way more difficult than coming out, there was no turning back. I bought a book called *From Wedded Wife to Lesbian Life* after my husband and I separated and I remember asking my partner, after reading the personal essays and looking at the pictures of the women therein, "Do I have to look so butch?"

She laughed, but at the same time there was this kind of strange unspoken thing happening. All of the trappings of femininity—makeup, heels, a little cleavage, the perfect accessories—became suspect to her. Was I going to leave her for a man? Was I really gay or just biding my time? Was some guy at work flirting with me? I'd been so happy and relieved to finally name my gay, but now I felt like the way I looked was, once again, interfering with who I was.

It was incredibly frustrating and at times infuriating. Heteronormativity, especially when it comes to feminine women, is the standard. And the fact that the assumptions came from both sides of the spectrum could definitely nudge a girl into giving up her favorite pair of heels forever.

But what I discovered in the process of discovering myself was that I still loved being a feminine girl. I loved the perfect pair of earrings or the shimmering necklace that accentuated my collarbone just right. I loved a simple blush, lipstick, mascara combo for every single day. I liked feeling pretty. Not for men. Not for women. Not for some societal standard, but for *me*.

I suppose, as girls, we have a choice. We can choose to rebel against the male gaze and stop wearing makeup. We can stop messing with our hair. We can wear clothes that hide our femininity. But what if you like all that girly stuff? What if that stuff fills you up on some fundamental level and you like looking in the mirror and seeing all of the *girl* that is you? Do we stop simply because eyes are watching? Or because other eyes say tone it down?

Some girls do. They find it easier to take their femininity down a notch to avoid the stares and assumptions or accusations. Some girls pick and choose the moments to let it shine and go all out only for a special occasion or a special person. Some girls choose to buck gender conventions and standards altogether. Each choice made from a place of personal power and desire is valid. But we should be able to own our femininity, if that's our choice, without risk and without reprise. And fear of, or actual, objectification should never be a reason to hide our truest selves. We simply have to remember we are *not* objects.

Our femininity is beautiful. The way we choose to dress, whether in pink and sparkles, plunging necklines and short skirts, or a men's department shirt and baggy jeans, isn't about sending some kind of message to the world. It's not saying *I want it* or *I'm vapid* or *Don't take me seriously*. It's about choosing the things that make us feel whole and complete and beautiful—inside and out.

So while we may never be able to avoid the male gaze or society's ideals of the right or wrong way to woman entirely, we can acknowledge that it's no one's right to cast eyes upon you and categorize you as an object. Dress how you want for you. Choose to be feminine but at the same time buck gender roles or sexuality assumptions if that's who you are. There's no single right way to girl. And no one has the prerogative to tell you how to do it or judge you for your choices.

Go out and roar.

EASTER OFFERING

Brandy Colbert

I suppose it's safe to say I never felt comfortable in my hometown.

Although I recognized feeling uncomfortable, when you're "the only one" for years and years, standing out simply because you're different becomes normal. I still noticed when heads whipped around to stare at me, the only brown face in the room time and time again. The murmurs in the background didn't escape me. But I learned how easy it is to become desensitized to ignorant comments from those who've never experienced being around a group of people who look nothing like them.

Simply put, I adapted. I had to.

Being a good student was part of adapting, because I couldn't give anyone a reason to look at me like I didn't belong or believe that I wasn't good enough. I consistently brought home As and Bs. There was no other option in my household, where I was raised by two parents who were born into Southern farming families and worked hard to give my older brother and me a comfortable, middle-class upbringing. My parents didn't often remind us of how far they'd come—there were no legendary talks about walking four miles to school in the snow. But we knew they'd grown up picking cotton in their parents' fields and sharing beds with multiple siblings and attending schools in rural Arkansas that had to be desegregated.

Though they seemed so far removed from that upbringing—to this day, I swear I've never heard either of my parents speak with a Southern accent—I thought of it frequently, and so I knew it was my job to behave well, achieve good grades, and make them proud.

History was always one of my least favorite classes, and one of my hardest-earned grades. The textbooks were so dry, even the most inquisitive students would find themselves nodding off after a few paragraphs. But I was probably in third grade when I realized how uncomfortable class was on the days we discussed Black history. It wasn't until much later that I realized it was also extremely troubling that I could pinpoint the *days* we talked about Black Americans out of a whole nine months of sitting in class. And we rarely talked about their contributions, which were pushed aside in favor of discussing the horrors of slavery and sanitizing the work of civil rights activists like Rosa Parks.

US history textbooks have generally been skewed toward the accomplishments of white men, but I always noticed one time of year when my fellow female classmates took particular interest: the story of the suffragettes.

Because I grew up in a predominantly white town, I've had many white female friends ever since I can remember. I was, of course, aware of our differences. When I was younger, I wanted to have long, silky hair like theirs as opposed to the kinky curls that were dutifully worked out of my head through any means necessary. I wanted boys to crush on me and ask me out, even though it was obvious that having a Black girlfriend was incredibly taboo where I lived.

The girls in my class were so proud when the history lesson focused on the suffragettes. "They gave us *all* the right to vote!" "They fought so hard for *women's* rights!" "They forced men to acknowledge them as *equals*!" Well, yes.

But.

Those same textbooks didn't discuss the full legacy of the suffragettes—including their racism. There was no paragraph detailing how Susan B. Anthony, perhaps one of the most famous advocates of women's voting rights, stated that "I will cut off this right arm of mine before I will ever work or demand the ballot for the Negro and not the woman."

In addition to disparaging all Black Americans with that comment, Anthony failed to recognize that Black women face oppression for not only their gender, but their race as well.

* * *

In 1906, a young white man and white woman claimed to have been attacked by two masked Black men in Springfield, Missouri. Horace Duncan and Fred Coker, two Black men, were arrested on suspicion of assault, robbery, and rape, though they could not have been recognized, as the assailants were said to be wearing masks. Despite being released after their white employer provided an alibi for the two coworkers and lifelong friends, Duncan and Coker were arrested that same evening on a separate charge of robbery by the white man who had accused them of the initial attack.

Not satisfied with their imprisonment, a lynch mob dragged Duncan and Coker from their cells in the middle of the night and took them down to the town square, where they were lynched from Gottfried Tower in front of an estimated crowd of three thousand. The mob later returned to the jail and removed Will Allen, who'd been accused of murdering a Confederate veteran. He was lynched at the same site as Duncan and Coker. Newspapers at the time reported that the onlookers took home pieces of the burned rope, clothes, and bones as keepsakes.

Prior to these lynchings, Black people thrived in Springfield. They were segregated from the white population, but they owned businesses, including the largest grocery store in town. They held office in city council and worked as attorneys, educators, dentists, and pharmacists. At the time, Springfield's Black population was around 10 percent, or 2,300 citizens.

After the lynchings, the Black population rapidly declined, quite nearly overnight. When I was growing up in Springfield in the 1980s and 1990s, the number of Black residents fluctuated between 2 and 3 percent.

Through the years, I'd read extensively about Emmett Till, the fourteen-year-old boy who was kidnapped and brutally murdered after being accused of whistling at a white woman in Mississippi. There were similarities between the cases, but the Springfield lynchings, which took place four decades prior to Till's murder, hit so close to home.

It broke my heart to learn that those acts of terror all but decimated the Black population in my hometown. My tears were primarily of mourning for those three men, who didn't deserve the fate they met on the town square that Easter weekend in 1906. But they were also tears of anger and regret. I felt like I'd been robbed of my chance to grow up with a large and successful Black community, all because of the false accusations of two white people who had nothing to lose.

Talking to my white friends about the suffragettes has always proved less than satisfying. When we were younger, I don't think anyone ever questioned my lack of enthusiasm directly, but I remember practicing the "If you can't say something nice . . ." rule around those discussions more often than not. Because even without knowing at the time that many of the suffragettes held racist ideals, something felt off. Why weren't Black or Native or

Latina or Asian women marching alongside them? Why were the only women whose names were mentioned in the history books white?

When it was clear that Hillary Clinton was to become the first female presidential candidate of the Democratic Party, I felt a vague sense of contentment. I'd never held a strong opinion about her either way, but I felt she was not only the most accomplished candidate, but extremely qualified in her own right. It was an easy decision to vote for her in the primaries.

As election season continued, I began to feel a deep division between what the majority of my white women friends were discussing over dinner and on social media and what I was personally feeling. While Clinton mostly represented the policies I felt were important, many of my friends were absolutely enamored with her. There were so many emotional posts about what a role model she was, how they'd dreamed of this moment forever, and how they were "with her" that I lost count. And as the months passed and their support became more vocal, I soon realized they felt like I had about the nomination and subsequent election of President Barack Obama.

I lived in Chicago at the time of Obama's first presidential campaign, but I chose to spend election night in my apartment alone, watching the results from under a blanket. When he was announced the winner, I let out a noise I've never heard before or since from myself—a shocked, elated, and relieved sort of strangled cry. This country that has so many unresolved horrors threaded through its fabric had done the unthinkable: it had elected its first Black president. I don't know if I'd ever been so proud of someone I'd never met. It felt like a huge and long-overdue victory for Black America.

Though I didn't feel that same level of excitement for Clinton, I was proud to vote for a woman in the primaries and general election. She may not know what it's like to be a Black woman, but I know what it is to be a woman, and I was well aware of how much opposition she'd faced to get where she was. This country is also long overdue for a woman president, and in those earlier days, I fully expected to see her ushered into the highest office.

I don't recall when I first learned about Fannie Lou Hamer. Much too late, as I found out about her on my own. In the years since graduating from college—where I took exactly one history class, the one needed to fulfill my general education requirement—I'd become quite interested in history. I could research what I wanted when I wanted, and it was all at my fingertips with instant access to the Internet.

Perhaps I stumbled upon Hamer when I wondered where the famous quote "I'm sick and tired of being sick and tired" came from. I was surprised to see a Black woman credited with the quote, and even more surprised to see that she'd been a civil rights activist, particularly focused on voting rights for Southern Black people, before she died. How could I know that quote and not have been taught where it came from? Why did we not learn about Hamer when we studied civil rights, instead of recycling tired paragraphs about Martin Luther King Jr. that excluded the full impact and intent of his activism?

Hamer resonated with me because she was fighting for the rights of my family. Like my parents, she was born in the South and worked in the fields. She was also from an enormous household—one that, with nineteen brothers and sisters, made my mother's thirteen-child family and my father's nine siblings pale in comparison. Though Hamer shared a generation with my grandparents, by the time my own parents were born in the early 1950s, Jim Crow laws were still prevalent in the South, and Hamer was fighting them hard.

She worked with the Student Nonviolent Coordinating Committee to seek equality through civil disobedience and helped organize Freedom Summer in 1964, a voting registration project in Mississippi. She was also a founding member of the Mississippi Freedom Democratic Party and ran for Congress, though her bid was unsuccessful. Hamer was a philanthropist, donating food and clothing to poor families in her hometown community, and cofounded the National Women's Political Caucus.

One evening a few years ago, I watched video of Hamer at the 1964 Democratic National Convention, where she testified to challenge the appointment of all-white Mississippi delegates. I couldn't look away as she sat poised and calm in her printed cotton dress, Southern accent strong as she matter-of-factly described her beating in a Mississippi jail after being arrested with a group for trying "to register to become first-class citizens." President Lyndon B. Johnson attempted to block Hamer's speech from television by holding an impromptu press conference, but he was unsuccessful. Her impactful testimony was broadcast by several evening news programs, providing her with an even larger stage to tell her story.

"I question America," Hamer said at the end of her speech. "Is this America, the land of the free and the home of the brave, where we have to sleep with our telephones off of the hooks because our lives be threatened daily, because we want to live as decent human beings, in America?"

My hometown newspaper published an article in 2006 to commemorate the hundred-year anniversary of the triple lynching of Horace Duncan, Fred Coker, and Will Allen. I was in my midtwenties, living in my adopted hometown of Los Angeles, and read it alone in my bedroom, huddled in front of my laptop with tears streaming down my face. It was hard to work through my emotions at the time, but years later I would cycle through the same set of feelings after watching Steve McQueen's *12 Years a Slave*, the true story of Solomon Northup, a freed Black man who was kidnapped and sold into slavery: shock, horror, extreme rage, and hopelessness.

I also felt, in both instances, that it would be a long time before I could face a white person without projecting my anger onto them. That wasn't fair, but it was honest.

At the time I read about my hometown's shameful history, I was sharing an apartment with two white women who were also my close friends. Both had blond hair and blue eyes; they could be mistaken for sisters, and I used to joke about how different their Nordic features looked in comparison to mine. I was happy with the way I looked by then, having learned to love my brown skin that bronzed with a noticeable glow when I spent time in the sun, and even embracing the natural curls of my hair, which I'd been conditioned to dislike for most of my life. But it was instinct, going back to my days of being the only one—pointing out my differences before someone could do it for me.

My white women friends in Los Angeles were proud progressives, and my roommates were no exception. They had racially and sexually diverse friend groups and coworkers. They welcomed inclusivity and were willing to have uncomfortable, open talks about race. But as white women, they couldn't quite grasp how my Blackness intersected with my gender.

I locked myself in my room when the aftermath of Hurricane Katrina permeated news reports because I was so angry at how Black people in New Orleans were abandoned by our government. My roommates didn't understand that although, like them, I was far away and had no family living there, the people in the devastated communities of New Orleans felt like my brothers and sisters. I knew what it was like to feel that nobody cared about your well-being simply because of your skin color, and I was seeing it play out on national TV.

There was a local bar up the street where my roommates and I were, admittedly, regulars. The crowd was pretty typical of the neighborhood, with mostly young, white professionals gathering to have drinks with friends. One night, I was shocked to see two Black men sitting with a group at a table in the corner. They noticed me, too, and in a move that still makes me laugh to this day, one of them sent his friend over to say my presence was requested at their table. I don't take orders from many people, and especially not strange men, so I shook my head and continued talking to my friends. Later that night, I was going over the incident with my roommates, annoyed and wondering what would possess someone to "approach" a woman like that. A few moments later one of my roommates said, "Maybe he was intimidated because you were with two white women."

It was my second shock of the night. Though it wasn't an excuse for sending someone else to do his bidding, I could see intimidation being a factor—for a number of reasons. Maybe he thought I was pretty . . . or he was painfully shy around strange women . . . or he didn't want to approach me because I was with *friends*. But being intimidated because those friends were *white* women? I was offended that she'd had that thought and that she had been careless enough to say so in front of me. I was offended, but instead of confronting her, I shut down the conversation and went to bed. I was offended, and I was tired of feeling like I constantly had to be on alert with people who were ostensibly on my side.

* * *

Hillary Clinton won the popular vote in the 2016 presidential election but failed to win the electoral college. I was upset when she lost, but I wasn't surprised. Though support for her had been strong in my circles, clearly a large part of the country did not feel she was the best candidate. And as cynical as it sounds, I personally believed our luck had run out after the country voted a Black man into office for two consecutive terms. What I saw as the inevitable backlash reminded me of the vitriol spewed by suffragettes like Susan B. Anthony, who were enraged that Black men had been allowed to vote before white women.

I'm not sure I've ever seen my white friends, particularly the women, so distressed. Suddenly, people who had never even acknowledged activism for marginalized groups were taking to the streets, posting selfies from protests around the country. They had gotten a taste of the deep injustice that marginalized people in the United States have experienced for centuries and were determined to do something about it.

I was included on group texts with well-meaning friends who were too blinded by their newly felt oppression to realize that many other groups had more to lose than them. I muted and eventually removed myself from the texts because I didn't have the energy—nor was it my responsibility—to console them. I knew before I was ten years old what it felt like to have racial slurs hurled at me, and to have people who knew nothing about me assume my parents couldn't afford to take me out for cheeseburgers, and to have white parents hustle their kids out of the hotel pool when my family was on vacation in Orlando because I wanted to swim, too, and I had brown skin.

Suddenly, in their thirties and forties, my white women friends realized how it felt to know that no matter how hard you worked and how much you hoped, you could still lose horribly. Because I was a woman, these friends automatically thought to include me in their complaints about the rampant sexism and disregard for women's rights. They weren't wrong—I feel sickened by it, too. But they failed to see that this isn't a new feeling for me, just an additional struggle in my life. They wanted support, and I was irritated that the same people who chose to say and do nothing to protest the multiple murders and mistreatment of Black people caught on film in the last several years were looking for comfort from marginalized communities.

Perhaps the most upsetting part of the election for me was learning that 53 percent of white women voted for Clinton's opponent—a man who had a strong history of discrimination against Black people and held no regard for the lives of immigrants and Muslims, who openly mocked a disabled reporter, and who surrounded himself with shameless bigots. If all of that combined didn't convince them not to vote for him, I was sure the last straw would be when he was caught on tape boasting about sexually assaulting women—*white* women.

There was no last straw.

* * *

A couple months after the election, a decade-old interview with the woman who had accused Emmett Till, the teenager murdered in Mississippi, of flirting with her, was released. The suspects of the murder (the woman's husband and his half brother) had been acquitted in 1955. In 2007, Carolyn Bryant, who went into hiding after the trial, admitted to a historian that she had lied in court about her contact with Till. "Nothing that boy did could ever justify what happened to him," she declared.

But it was much, much too late. Her regret couldn't have saved him back then, but perhaps it could have served him justice in court.

Nobody really talks about the lynchings in my hometown. They weren't a part of our history lessons growing up, and while I'm not sure how many people are aware of the story, those who are seem profoundly uncomfortable when the topic surfaces.

Though I didn't read the details until I was much older, there were always vague murmurings around town. In the aftermath, the lynchings were crudely referred to as the "Easter Offering"; they made the front page of several newspapers around the country and have been covered in books, as well. The tower used for the hangings, which featured an iron replica of the Statue of Liberty, was destroyed a few years afterward.

I attended college in my hometown and used to walk through the square quite often. I must have crossed through the exact site of the lynchings dozens of times—on the way to my internship at the city's business journal, which had likely never employed a Black editor, or huddled with a giggling group of my white friends as we stretched across the sidewalk after nightfall, heading to our favorite bars and clubs.

In August 2002, the city voted to erect a bronze plaque in the square to commemorate the lynchings, despite controversy. The plaque measures about four inches by twelve inches, and I've heard it's so small that it can be easily missed, even if you're looking for it.

I haven't seen it. I moved to Los Angeles in January of the year it was installed, and though I've returned many times to visit family, I haven't made the trip to the square. I will go see it someday. It feels, somehow, like the best way to pay my respects to Horace Duncan, Fred Coker, and Will Allen.

Maybe then I won't feel so much resentment at the fact that my hometown became a nearly all-white city not by circumstance but by force.

Perhaps then I can come to terms with the fact that although our country is fraught with racial tension and division to this day, there are people who eventually seek to acknowledge the wrongs of the past.

There are people who won't let us forget, no matter how small the reminder.

I left my hometown sixteen years ago, and I continue to struggle with my memories. It's difficult to have warm, fuzzy feelings about a place that, as a whole, never seemed that welcoming. I am still friends today with several people I met there, and the memories of my childhood are more fond than unpleasant. Since moving away, I've lived in Los Angeles, Chicago, and Los Angeles again. I've always said Springfield was a nice place to grow up, and it was—because I was strong enough to handle it. Or maybe I just adapted.

Either way, I grew a thick skin that serves me well today. The ignorance, microaggressions, and blatant racism still hurt, but at this point in my life it's rare that I'm confronted with a situation I've never dealt with. Now I face these experiences with the confidence of knowing who I am, not mired in worrying about how other people view me. I have the language to express myself when I see or experience injustice, and I use it.

In the days, weeks, and months after the election, a common refrain was that people were numb. They didn't know how to feel when it was exceedingly clear that the foundation of this country they held so dear was in jeopardy. They didn't know how to complete their everyday tasks or feel okay about relaxing when human rights were at stake.

I don't know how to make them feel better about their sudden awakening, but I strive to use Fannie Lou Hamer as a role model—a woman who fought for the rights of Black people, women, and poor people because she knew what it was to live as a poor Black woman.

I know that as a Black woman, I will keep doing what I've been doing my whole life: I will fight for the voiceless and those who are less privileged than me. I will fight even when I am uncomfortable. I will fight to make myself seen and heard.

I will fight until there is no longer a need.

TRUMPS AND TRUNCHBULLS

Alexandra Duncan

When I was growing up, one of my favorite books was Roald Dahl's *Matilda*. Not just because the title character has telekinesis, which I think we can all agree is pretty sweet, but because of the villain, Miss Trunchbull. Miss Trunchbull is the sadistic headmistress of Matilda's school, Crunchem Hall. She keeps a medieval torture device called an iron maiden in her office and devises bizarre ways to punish her students for minor infractions or imagined slights, such as flinging them over fences by their braids or force-feeding them chocolate cake until they burst. She is able to get away with this because her behavior is so outlandish that none of the parents believe it when the children complain.

Don't get me wrong, I hated Miss Trunchbull. But I was

grateful for her existence, because she gave me a way to frame the abuse and gaslighting that was going on in my own home. My Trunchbull, like the one in the book, always told me I was exaggerating or making things up, always saying—in so many words—that no one would believe me about the things he did. He was a respected member of the community, after all. A family man. Powerful. Religious. And me? I was just a kid whose dad had run off and left her mom alone. Then a teenager who had better watch her smart mouth. Then a young woman whose word could be dismissed because the fact that she wrote novels for a living meant the stories she finally told her mother were just more "creative writing."

"I don't remember that" was his refrain when confronted with accounts of his behavior.

The time I tried to catch my baby sister when she was falling and he insisted I pushed her, then made my mother spank me as punishment?

"I would never have done that."

The time he turned on pornography in front of me and my brother?

"That never happened," he would have said. "And if it did, why didn't you leave the room?"

The million cutting comments? *You should be a country singer, since you're so good at whining. You're too smart to be so stupid. That's going straight to your waistline. Are you gay?*

"If I said those things, why didn't you tease me back?"

89

The one time I did talk back to him and he told me he'd make my life a living hell?

"I don't remember that."

End of conversation. If he didn't remember it, it hadn't happened.

This tactic is called gaslighting. The term comes from a 1944 movie about a man who tries to convince his wife she's going insane. He moves objects in their home, hides her belongings, and dims the gas lights, all the while insisting that the changes aren't happening, or if they are, she is the one responsible for them. The term has come to describe a common pattern of behavior among abusers and emotional manipulators. Sometimes it shows up as the abuser convincing his victim that she caused or deserved whatever terrible thing happened to her. Sometimes it's the abuser denying that he did the terrible thing at all. And sometimes it's the abuser preemptively accusing his victim of exactly the terrible thing he himself is guilty of in order to undermine her ability to call him out on it.

Gaslighting sounds like a sophisticated technique, but it's not. All it requires is a convincing facsimile of conviction and the mere suggestion that reality is not what it seems. If the abuser shouts his Bizarro-World version of events loudly enough and often enough, at least some people will believe it, and that will make his victims second-guess themselves. That's the real terror of gaslighting—that your sense of reality begins to warp and bend until you're excusing the abuser and doing his work for him.

It's my fault. If I hadn't been so slow to finish raking the lawn, if I had said yes, sir *when I answered, instead of just* yes, *he would have let me out to see my friends. He wouldn't have stopped me from going to my great-grandmother's one hundredth birthday party.*

It's not like he hit me . . . except for that time when he slapped the dish towel against me so hard it stung. Or the time he spanked me because I was trying to hug him good night and accidentally knelt on his groin. But those don't count. It's not like it was a regular thing.

It's not like he raped me or anything. He only pinched my butt. And that one time, when I was in college and he tried to get me to kiss my friend on the lips so he could take our picture. (And, and, and . . .) But he was just teasing. He didn't know those things were inappropriate. I'm overreacting.

Then when they talk at school about abused women and kids you think, *Those poor women. Those poor kids. That's not me.*

When I was in high school I thought sexism was over, because my parents had me do boy chores like mowing the lawn and the riot grrrl ethos of the early nineties had been commodified and repackaged as the Spice Girls. Women could be astronauts! Barbie was a doctor! Girl power! My mother and her friends all worked, and I didn't notice until later that for the most part, they were confined to a very specific set of careers: nurse, teacher, secretary. They were smart women. They cared about their kids and their church, so wasn't it natural that they were the first ones to be asked to drop work obligations when the kids were sick or the church needed volunteers? Women were innately better with kids, so wasn't it natural that they—and I—should be the ones asked to miss out on the church service in order to watch the nursery?

And so, whenever someone underestimated me or talked over me at school or work or church, I ascribed it to something else.

It's because I'm young, I told myself. *When I'm older, they'll take me more seriously.*

Or, *It's because I'm new here. Once I've proved myself, they'll listen.*

Or sometimes, *I must not be adding anything to the conversation. If I had something smart to say, they would pay attention.*

But I got older, I gained experience, I proved myself time and time again, and things didn't change. I still tried to write off all of it as isolated incidents. One boss assigned me, the only woman on his staff, to clean the restrooms at work, despite some of the men in my same position being hired after me. He stood over me and nitpicked my work. He shouted at me for not working fast enough. I cried in my car every day at lunch until one of my coworkers pointed out that he was singling me out for this treatment. I left, but my next boss deliberately offered me a salary below the pay grade for the job. I worked weekends and holidays. I took a second job to make ends meet.

"Your husband works, doesn't he?" my boss asked one time when I mentioned my second job.

I didn't find out that I was being underpaid for two years, and by then there was nothing I could do about it. No one else did the same job as me, so I couldn't prove they'd underpaid me because of my gender. Besides, this was the early 2000s. Sexism wasn't a thing anymore, right?

The tipping point for me came when I entered my thirties, had several books published, was managing a public library branch, and yet still had men refer to me as "kiddo," "that little black-haired girl," and simply "girl." When a pawnshop was selling DVDs stolen from the library, I had to threaten to have a male colleague come to the shop before they would take me seriously and return the disks. When a patron had a computer question, a male coworker had to repeat my advice verbatim before the man would take it. A tax clinic aide told me I couldn't put my name first on my husband's and my joint tax return, even though I was the primary breadwinner and had prepared the tax forms she was checking over. A police officer initially assumed I was at fault when a man rear-ended me and totaled my car at a stoplight. A doctor wouldn't take the time to figure out why I was in excru-ciating abdominal pain; later I talked to some female friends and realized I'd probably had a burst ovarian cyst—a relatively com-mon problem for women, but one that can lead to complications or be a sign of other, more serious conditions. And on and on. The catcalls. The condescension. Being told to smile when my grand-mother had just died. All of those small things added up and up and up, and suddenly I realized: It wasn't me. This was bullshit.

Sometimes it's hard to maintain that clarity of vision. Living as a woman in our society is like living with an abuser, a Trunchbull. He tells you you're overreacting. He tells you your memory of the way things happened can't be trusted. He says you're being hysterical, and this is proof that women are too unstable to be in charge of anything. Except housework. And childcare. Women are just naturally better at those things, after all. *(Why can't you take a compliment?)* He makes you doubt yourself, police yourself, guard your anger. Because if you let a sliver of that rage show, even for a second, he'll claim you're the one abusing him. *Feminazi! Misandrist! Take the red pill!*

He pretends to side with the men in our lives, but in reality he's abusing them, too. *Don't let anyone ever see you cry. Aren't you man enough? You have to talk to your wife before you buy a car? Man, you're pussy-whipped.* And so he uses them, tries to convince them they won't be mocked so long as they keep themselves at a distance from anything feminine. He sets us against each other so that we'll be too blinded to see what he's doing to us. And often our Trunchbull's messages are so ingrained in our culture that we can't recognize there's anything wrong with them.

Of course men get paid more. They have families to support.

No one's stopping women from doing whatever job they want. The only reason they get paid less than men is that they drop out of the workforce to have babies.

What are you bitching about? It's not like you live in one of those countries where women can't drive.

Women objectify men, too. Everyone does it. Stop acting like a victim.

If she wanted anyone to believe her, she wouldn't have gotten drunk at that party.

You only dress like that if you want attention.

It can't be rape if he's your husband.

Why don't you smile?

On most days I don't think about my Trunchbull or the things he did. I cut off contact with him about five years ago, and so have many of the other people in my family. I have a PTSD and major depression diagnosis, but I keep up with my therapy and antidepressants. I have a wonderful husband, great friends, and a full life.

But like many women who suffered at the hands of an abuser, I was reminded of him again when Donald Trump became the Republican presidential nominee in 2016. I've heard that some women, seeing him lurking behind Hillary Clinton in the second debate as she answered questions from the audience, felt that old terror coming back. That cold, tight feeling that comes over you when you see your Trunchbull's car in the driveway or hear him call your name. But for me, it was actually the third debate that made my stomach sink, because that's when I realized everyone was falling for the same gaslighting techniques my Trunchbull had used against me, only on a national stage.

In the debate, Clinton pointed out Trump's ties to Russia,

calling him Russian president Vladimir Putin's puppet.

Trump sputtered in response, "No puppet. You're the puppet."

I cheered for Clinton then. *Yes,* I thought. *Finally someone is exposing him for what he is.*

The CIA has since reported Russia interfered with our election to tip it in Trump's favor and the Justice Department has assigned special counsel Robert Mueller to investigate. As of this writing, Trump's national security advisor Michael Flynn has resigned and Attorney General Jeff Sessions has recused himself from investigating the situation, both because of their Russian connections. Trump's former campaign adviser Carter Page was put under surveillance by the FBI because of suspicions that he was an "agent of a foreign power." The president's son Donald Trump Jr. drew headlines when he revealed he had met with a Russian lawyer in June 2016 because she claimed to have damaging information about the Clinton campaign. And this is only what's happened by early 2018. Who knows what will be revealed by the time this book is released?

But as the debate continued that night, my stomach sank. *No one believes her,* I realized. I could feel it in the room. Like Miss Trunchbull picking up children by their braids, the things Trump had done were so outlandish, the accusations bounced right off of him and reflected on Clinton instead, playing into the tired old stereotype of the "hysterical woman" who is too crazy and emotional to be taken seriously.

It almost feels silly to call this tactic gaslighting, because any reasonable human should be able to see this sort of *I know you are, but what am I* routine for what it is, and yet . . .

And yet the country still elected Trump. And yet I still second-guess myself when I tell the story of what happened to me as a child and young woman. One of a gaslighter's favorite cards to play is *I'm the real victim here!* which goes right along with a related technique, accusing the actual victim of being the perpetrator.

"I never abused the kids," the everyday gaslighter says. "You just manipulated them into hating me."

"Calm down," he says when you're angry or crying. "We can discuss this when you're less emotional."

"You are witnessing the single greatest WITCH HUNT in American political history," tweets the president.

In politics or daily life, the recipe is the same—denial plus switching the role of the victim and the perpetrator. The accusation does damage all on its own, by making us question reality and distracting us from the actual issue, whether it's domestic abuse or Trump's Russian connections. We watch the news and read history books with the same skewed vision that let us say, *That's not me.*

How could the people there let this happen? we think. *I would have tried to stop it.*

But would we? What makes some people push back against their histories of abuse, break the cycle, and try to become the sort of person who protects others rather than abuses them? It would be so easy to decide the only way not to be a victim is to become an abuser. The Trumps and Trunchbulls of the world have the power, after all. So many people who are abused as children grow up to become abusers themselves.

I understand how it happens. I wish I didn't. When my husband and I first got married, we fought about the dumb, everyday things couples do, like the grocery bill and who was spending too much time on the computer. But when I opened my mouth, the words that came out were my Trunchbull's. I thought I had escaped him, but there was a part of him lodged in me, waiting there. All that rage bottled up inside me couldn't be unleashed on the person who deserved it, so it flew out at the wrong moment, at the wrong person. I was horrified. I had promised myself I would never be like my Trunchbull, that if I saw anyone being hurt the way I had been, I would do what no one did for me and speak up.

For a while I did an exceptionally good job of bottling up that rage, turning it inward and unleashing it only on myself, but that simply hurt my husband and the other people I loved in a different way. After it got bad enough that I stopped eating and started thinking I should drive into a tree because everyone in my life would be better off without me, I finally went to see a therapist. I had fought against taking antidepressants for years out of some misguided notion that they would turn me into a zombie. Instead, they literally saved my life.

In therapy, I learned to take care of myself. I learned that my anger wasn't fundamentally bad. Some of it was justified; I just had to learn how to channel it. One of the forces that has always driven me is the desire to protect people, especially other people vulnerable to the bullies and Trunchbulls of the world. So, I learned I could turn my anger into fierce love, a longer-burning fuel than rage.

So many people are gaslit and abused on a societal level, not only because of their gender, but because of their race, ethnicity, religion, sexual orientation, et cetera. Look at the Black Lives Matter movement, for example. Its goal is simply to convince the world that African-Americans' lives have the same fundamental value as people of other races, and that police and government officials should recognize that value. Yet BLM's detractors shout that the movement is a terrorist organization, that any crime committed by an African-American person was motivated by BLM, and that saying "Black Lives Matter" somehow means others' lives don't. It's classic gaslighting. The abuser shouts that they are the victim, feeding into the same lie that made Black Lives Matter necessary in the first place—that African-Americans are dangerous, subhuman criminals—in an attempt to muddy the waters and obscure the truth. If people hear it enough times, maybe they'll start to believe it, or at least think it's a reasonable opinion that deserves consideration. *Don't you care about free speech?*

This societal gaslighting becomes only more intense as people's identities overlap and combine. Being a white woman can be hard. Being a woman of color, harder still. Being a trans or lesbian woman of color, even more difficult. Add poverty, religious restrictions or prejudices, and access (or lack thereof) to education, and that matrix of pain and manipulation grows yet more complex. We can't know exactly what other people's pain is like, but we can listen and believe them when they say it hurts. We can try to stop whatever is causing it.

I wrote earlier that my family was religious and dedicated to our church. I don't call myself a Christian anymore. I can never trust a religious community after what my church allowed to happen under its nose and how they responded when someone finally told them about it. I suppose I'm agnostic, though when people hear that, they assume I'm a wishy-washy nihilist who sees no meaning in the world. But for me, agnosticism is a kind of faith. So many Christians I knew as a child and teenager were content to fold their hands and disengage from the world. *God has a plan,* they would say. *What happens in this life doesn't matter anyway. It will all be made right in the next.*

I don't believe that. I believe we have a responsibility to make things right in this life—right here, right now. I don't know if there is a heaven or if we get more than this life on earth. If there isn't an afterlife, if there isn't divine justice, that makes what happens here and now all the more critical. I think if we want to end the suffering in the world, we have to do it ourselves. We have to fight hate in all its forms—racism, homophobia, xenophobia, sexism, religious prejudice and extremism—tooth and nail, with fierce and lasting love. We have to stand up and use whatever energy and privilege we have to fight the Trumps and the Trunchbulls, especially now that we have a gaslighter in chief making people's lives even more difficult and frightening. We have to clear our eyes and speak the truth.

So here is what I promise, and what I hope you'll promise, too: I will do my part. I will work quietly and steadily, taking every opportunity I reasonably can to mitigate the enormous hurt in the world. I will speak up when need be. I will listen when others are talking about their pain, and I will believe them. I will pitch in and volunteer. I will take care of myself so I can keep going. I will probably mess up, but when I do, I will get back up and try again. No single one of us is going to save the world. But all of us might.

TINY BATTLES

Maurene Goo

I.

When I was little, I kept a diary with holes ripped through the pages from all the times I scratched so hard the pen poked through—a small angry fist clutching my Keroppi pen because all my friends had ditched me. Because they said "loser" under their breaths when I walked by their desks to do a math problem on the board. Later, in high school, my anger was fueled by the injustice that the boys I loved with the heat of a thousand suns didn't know I existed, by the delirious all-nighters I pulled so that I could get into a respectable college like the good Korean daughter I was, by the intense frustrations with my parents who just didn't understand *any* of it.

Anger coursed through me like water in a burst pipe—the

rage spewing everywhere, uncontrolled and unfocused. Hitting everything in its path.

How many times did I regret, the second after I did it, throwing a desk lamp onto the floor? How many pillowcases were left moldering under the constant assault of tears and saliva from my openmouthed screams?

I am an angry person and have always been this way. My Facebook profile used to say, "I never take the high road." What was the point? Passivity was almost offensive to me. I didn't understand people who just "let things go." *Let it go*? What the actual fuck does that *mean*?

II.

My high school was the school that you never saw in movies or on TV: a mix of immigrants and children of immigrants from all over the globe—Armenia, Mexico, El Salvador, Iran, Taiwan, the Philippines, Korea, et cetera. I could count the number of white kids at my entire school on one hand.

In this Benetton ad of a high school, my best girl friends were on the volleyball team. They wore tight little shorts and had sturdy legs while I sat in the bleachers wearing oversized sweatshirts to cover up my skeletal frame. It didn't matter—what I lacked in body mass I made up for with my huge mouth. I cheered aggressively for my friends and my school, like a girl possessed. I loved picking fights with fans from the opposing team, loved slinging insults at their players. It was the perfect pastime for someone who was competitive but had zero athletic ability.

One day we played against a high school that I shall charitably call Homogenous High. It was a team of blond ponytails and last names that were easy for American mouths to pronounce.

So there we were at this game—a pretty run-of-the-mill game since Homogenous High was in our school district and we played them often—when the kid next to me on the bleachers starts rummaging through his duffel bag. I glance over at him: *blond water-polo-player-looking fool*. Whatever. I feel mild irritation at all the rummaging noises but nothing worse than that. But before I can focus back on the game, I see him pull out an American flag.

I get that prickly feeling on the back of my neck, that instant temperature rise. My heart starts beating just a bit quicker. Even before he speaks a word, I know why that flag is there.

He unfurls it, and it's as wide as his arm span. Then he, and the kids next to him, start chanting, "USA! USA!" People look over, confused and annoyed. But then they turn back to the game.

I stare. I stare so hard.

Finally, I say to him, "What the hell is that supposed to mean?" The words come out fast. I'm not thinking of their consequences.

He won't even look at me, but he cracks this shit-eating

grin as he keeps his eyes straight ahead. "We're cheering for America."

"Stop it."

"Why? If you're American, you shouldn't mind. Don't you like America?"

By this point, people are looking at us, and I know that I'm red-faced and my voice is raised while his cronies laugh. An emotional teenage girl surrounded by chill dudes laughing. He keeps that flag waving. Absolutely shameless. So assured of his place in this gym, this city, this country.

I want to rip it out of his hands and make him eat it. I want to throw myself into his body so that we both go crashing down the bleachers. I want to scream, *YOU ARE BEING RACIST*. But the words needed to connect this act with racism are hard for me to find; I don't have the vocabulary nor the map for that yet.

Instead, I just hurl impotent obscenities at him that make him laugh. The game goes on and no one else speaks up. I feel completely alone in my rage.

I'm in a parking lot with my Asian-American girlfriends. We're giggling because I accidentally drove into the parking lot the wrong way and had to do some clunky maneuvering to get into a spot. We're walking toward a Mexican restaurant when we hear a male voice say, "I guess it's true that Asians can't drive." It's a middle-aged white man sitting in his car, watching us, a smile under his greasy mustache.

Screaming ensues. He continues to smile. Our dinner is ruined.

Even decades later I am careful of how I drive—I spent hours learning to parallel park until I could do it blindfolded. I drive fast and well because I refuse to be the bad Asian woman driver stereotype.

IV.

It's college now, and I am a little drunk with my friends. We start telling dumb jokes, laughing at each one. Then one of them says, "Hey, I have a good racist joke." I look at my friends—one white, one half Brazilian, several Chinese, one Mexican, two Persian, one Vietnamese. "What kind of racist joke?" I ask my friend uneasily.

"About Black people."

I tell him, "Fuck no. Don't tell a racist joke about Black people."

"Why not?"

This question begins an hours-long debate between me and one particular guy, the lone white dude. Like many times in my life, I don't hesitate to take the bait. This guy, he's like a lot of guys I meet in life. The kind that hate girls like me, that feel threatened and irritated by girls with strong opinions. I'm like a pebble in their shoe and their ego cannot take it. You know that guy. Most people ignore him. Not me.

And so I delve into the impossible waters of defining racism, but I am not equipped with the tools to articulate my thoughts about privilege. So I yell in anger. And I do the thing that I hate doing as a girl—I cry in frustration when they don't get it. I accuse Lone White Guy, who is my most ardent challenger, of being racist. It's loaded, but it's true. My head just about implodes when he says, "Black people should just wait for equality to happen naturally." I am angry, but I also feel sorry for him. That his life is so small, that he has had such little exposure to oppression and injustice, that he actually believes this. At this moment, my anger is balanced by a feeling of gratitude for the family and city that I was born into.

Later, when we've all left the red Solo cups behind, my friends thank me for speaking up. Their silence, which I interpreted as damning, was just discomfort and fear. Their thanks is like a balm.

V.

I leave California and go to graduate school in Boston. I'm not there to get an MFA in creative writing, but I take some literature classes with people who are. At first I'm comfortable in these classes—I have loved, known, lived in books my entire life. I've read everything. I can write critical essays dissecting literature in my sleep. I'm grateful for that confidence because I am the only person of color in these classes. In almost all my classes. Almost in my entire program. But after a while it's clear that I'm too irreverent. I don't take literature as seriously as them. I like talking about books, but I also don't name-drop Cheever in earnest. This makes me uncomfortable because I feel the pressure of needing to excel as the only nonwhite student. And because I'm a woman in a male-dominated class of full of little Hemingways in training. I need to prove that I am not in these classes by accident, that I knew what I was signing up for.

One evening in a lit class, we're talking about a popular memoir by a Black writer that had just been exposed as fiction written by a white woman. For me, being repulsed by this is natural; that is the normal reaction. For these guys, it's not. And I'm holding back because by this point the rage no longer runs through a burst pipe, but a sturdier one with some small leaks. (The pipe has been patched up by various things: the knowledge that people get shot on LA freeways over road rage, understanding that holding on to certain angers triggered my chronic anxiety and was toxic, and learning the hard way that explosive anger wasn't always productive.)

I listen to people as they are in agreement about this thing: that being a writer, an *artiste*, means you can write about anything. It's so entitled and clueless and I am conspicuously silent.

To speak or not to speak? To make everyone uncomfortable or to keep everyone feeling safe and cozy?

But when it starts to feel ridiculous, I speak, tentatively, knowing exactly who I am in that class. "I don't know. I think I understand why writing from the perspective of another culture might be a sensitive issue." (I was probably not this concise, probably stammering.) It is the most gentle, coddling way I can think of to express my views.

The biggest blowhard in the class, this fool who once told me with a straight face that New Hampshire had better Mexican food than California, this guy says, "I disagree. I can write about a Black man's experiences just as well as a Black person."

The silence is so thick, so loaded with discomfort and cowardice, that I also find myself speechless. (Oh, to have, as writer Sarah Hagi said, the confidence of a mediocre white man!)

It's only later, when I'm buzzing with anger on the train ride home, that I fully comprehend the shittiness of the position I had been in. That nothing I could have said wouldn't sound like hysterics from an overly sensitive Asian girl. Nothing short of MLK Jr.–level articulation would have shamed me as the Ambassador of All People of Color in Literature Programs.

I've had my culture appropriated and misrepresented my entire life. I know why one should be careful and thoughtful. Writers *can* write what they want, but I also know that they can, rightfully, be criticized for doing it poorly.

Years after this class, a white woman, bestselling author

Lionel Shriver, will walk onto a stage wearing a sombrero and basically proclaim the same thing as that bozo in my class. That as writers, we can write whatever we want—that awareness of cultural appropriation and good representation are stifling to the creative process. But by then I'm a published author and have finally found the words to rip literary entitlement like that to shreds. Step right up, folks. Ask me about the importance of diversity in literature and I promise this time I won't keep silent.

VI.

There are permanent lines in my forehead that I discovered after growing out my bangs.

"Your face is going to stay that way."

Grandma, you were right. My constant bitchface has now gifted me with these markers of my ragey time on earth.

Why am I reliving painful memories and listing grievances, each like a whisper out of Arya Stark's mouth as she falls asleep at night, like a promise of revenge?

Maybe it's because I'm Korean-American. Koreans believe we have *han*. It's hard as hell to describe. It's not a characteristic of Koreans as much as a concept that they feel is specific to their history and culture.

A quick and lazy Google search had this to say, on Wikipedia:

Han *or* **Haan** *is a concept in Korean culture
attributed as a unique Korean cultural trait which has
resulted from Korea's frequent exposure to invasions
by overwhelming foreign powers.* **Han** *denotes a
collective feeling of oppression and isolation in the
face of insurmountable odds . . . It connotes aspects of
lament and unavenged injustice.*

In her book, *The Birth of Korean Cool*, journalist Euny Hong says:

*The result of all this abuse is a culturally specific,
ultra-distilled form of rage, which Koreans call*
han *. . . By definition, only Koreans have* **han**,
*which arises from the fact that the universe can
never pay off this debt to them, not ever . . .*
. . . But Koreans do not consider han *to be a
drawback. It's not on the list of traits they want to
change about themselves.*

I actually discovered the concept of *han* by reading Hong's
book. My parents never mentioned it, I would guess because it's
so ingrained in the culture that there's no reason to explain it. If
you're Korean, you're born with it, just like you're born with the
burning desire to root for any professional sports team with a
single Korean player on it. So when I read Hong's chapter on *han*,
I felt like the wind was knocked out of me. *That's it.* I recognized

han on a molecular level—especially the part about "unavenged injustice." As mentioned earlier, in all of these stories I've just told, there was never enough justice doled out to satisfy me.

Because there's an alternate ending for each story:

The kid at the volleyball game gets expelled and is forced to watch *El Norte* on repeat until he cries blood.

The man in the parking lot keeps laughing until his car explodes to smithereens.

The racist joke teller fails out of college because he had no critical thinking skills and becomes a heroin addict—sad.

The smug MFA guy is forced to share a stage with Ta-Nehisi Coates, discussing how he could write about the Black experience better than him. And then literally shits his pants in front of me.

Alas.

I'm a firm believer in #noregrets. And in each of those instances, I found myself growing as a debater, a fighter. I leveled up each time someone was sexist, racist, or a delightful combination of both. It adds another little metal plate to the armor I wear every day.

VII.

I understand that there is a spectrum of anger. I don't want to punch a woman in line at the grocery store for taking too long counting her change. I want to have civil conversations on

heated topics without resorting to screaming and calling someone an asshole, which is what I did in high school and in college
fighting with those boys. And I certainly don't want friends and
family to fear confrontation with me.

After years of fights and arguments, I've learned how best
to communicate my anger, how to make my point effectively
and, in the best of cases, be persuasive. Having a husband with
the disposition of a monk helps. Therapy helps. And having a
proper outlet—my writing—has been the most helpful of all.

So now, when used wisely, I've discovered my anger is an
immensely satisfying weapon during battle—these personal,
tinier battles set against the backdrop of bigger battles that we all
need to fight against systemic racism and sexism. So I'm willing
to harness this rage, my *han*, and do something with it.

Because ever since November 8, 2016, there's a lot to be
angry about.

This last election opened a whole new facet of rage in me I
didn't know existed. Those unjust oppressions passed on to me
from my ancestors? They now take on the form of the person in
charge of my country. My home.

Seeing the stark differences between my reaction to the election and some of my Black, LGBTQ, and disabled friends com-
pounded it. They weren't as shocked as me. Their battles have
not been as tiny as mine, and many of them have always been
battle-ready, whether they wanted to be or not.

Now when I wake up angry because our basic tenets of

democracy are being threatened, I take that anger straight to my phone and call my representatives. It's the fuel that keeps me going when I'm fatigued by the news, when I feel helpless. If I see something idiotic on someone's Facebook wall—whether it's someone's great-uncle or a close friend—I'll speak up. I will tell the truth, even if it pushes them to a place of discomfort, so that they are forced to face their wrongness. My anger now courses through a very well-functioning pipe and I've installed a couple of convenient faucet handles.

VIII.

One night, unmoored and unemployed after graduating college, I started writing a story about a girl. A Korean-American teenager who always says what's on her mind and tries to do the right thing. Vulnerable yet fearless. I worked on this story on and off for a long time, over many years. Her voice was always in my head, urging me to sit in front of my computer and write her thoughts down.

> *I, for one, am looking forward to growing a year dumber through my abysmal California public school education.*

Heh heh.

Now I had to go to the stupid dance and find a stupid damn date.

Then many years later, someone wants to buy this story and make it into a book.

Since You Asked . . . , my first novel, was the culmination of years and years of rage. Rage that had no outlet. Rage that sometimes shamed me or got me into trouble. Maybe it's not so obvious when you read it, but it's there. Anger was the seed that book came from. It finally had somewhere to go.

I continue to write about teen girls. Not all my girls are angry. Some are those even-keeled types who mystify me. But I almost always write about Korean-American girls. I give them a voice in my novels because my readers are living in a world that is, sadly, not so different from the one I grew up in. We still live in a world where people will underestimate you because you are a girl, because you look different from them, because your parents are immigrants, because you worship differently, because you like girls instead of boys, because you're in a wheelchair, because you have to take medication to get through the day. These people who keep us on the margins, they think we will not fight back.

But those people are wrong. Those people can go fuck themselves.

Rage has empowered me, and I give you permission to let it empower you.

THESE WORDS ARE MINE

Stephanie Kuehnert

I had just turned fourteen when a boy touched me against my wishes for the first time. He was sixteen or maybe seventeen, from the small town where my friend and I were visiting her mom. One of the cute boys down the hill that my friend's mom gushed about. Brothers, she exclaimed. And they were excited to hang out with us. And did she mention cute? They were really cute.

Boys didn't notice us back home in the Chicago suburbs. We both had mega crushes that we'd nursed through eighth grade. In our heads, we were already dating those guys. We would marry them someday—tarot, horoscopes, and the Ouija board had all confirmed this. But, of course, the reality was we didn't even know if we'd see those boys again in our new, giant high school. So why not check out these other boys? These older boys. These boys who'd think we were cool just because we were from Chicago (well, close enough). Who could drive and take us on adventures. Who were "really cute," according to my friend's mom.

They were not cute. Not by our 1993, grunge-and-MTV-worshipping standards. They had mullets. They called our hero, Kurt Cobain, who *actually* was cute, the F word that neither of us would use. We would nickname them the Bon Jovi brothers. That was too kind, an insult to Bon Jovi.

But they could drive, we were bored, and my friend's mom had already set this whole thing in motion. We were to go out with them. We felt we had no choice.

They had a pickup truck. The two of us, the two of them, their younger brother, and their friend all rode to a pool hall in a nearby, slightly bigger town. On the way to the pool hall, I think we rode in the cab. I don't really remember. I also don't remember what the pool hall looked like. Smoky and dim, I imagine. I know that even though I was unimpressed by the boys and the banter that I'm sure they thought made them sound cool, I was still excited to be on this adventure—one I knew my own mother would never let me take. I also felt like I had some power over the boys because when they said that F word that I hated, I would glare and they would apologize.

Any feeling of power vanished the moment one of the brothers decided to show me how to hold the pool cue and very obviously, very intentionally groped my breast in the process. He smiled as he did it. That I remember. I think he probably said something too, some line that he thought was funny or slick, that let the rest of the guys know he had touched my boob and what it was like. I could tell that he thought I should laugh, that I should be turned on and let him touch me more.

I felt like I'd been hit by the stomach flu. I was nauseous. The room was too loud, too smoky. It was closing in and I was trapped. I didn't know how far I was from my friend's mom's house. This was exactly why my own mother would not have let me go on such an adventure. I hated that she was right, but I'd never wished harder for her to magically appear.

Of course she didn't. My friend's mother was not at home, and since cell phones weren't a common thing yet, we had no way to reach her and ask for a ride. We had no choice but to continue with these boys, hoping that it wouldn't get too much worse and that they would eventually take us home.

After the pool hall, we insisted on riding in the back of the truck, hoping for more space, more air. But since it was windy, it gave the boys (who'd decided to ride in back with us, of course) a reason to put their arms around us. Faux chivalry. "We don't want you to be cold." I'd invented a boyfriend by that point. It was my crush, except instead of sharing that he drew and played guitar, I said he was on the wrestling team. As if this boyfriend could somehow defend me from a thousand miles away. As if, I would reflect a couple years later, boyfriends would protect or defend you. It didn't help anyway. The twins' friend still stuck his hand up my cutoff shorts to "see how loose they were."

My friend did not invent a boyfriend because her mom had already told these boys she was single, so when the twin who groped me asked her out, she felt obligated to say yes. We were trapped in the back of a pickup going sixty miles per hour. We wanted to go home. We were fourteen and had never been asked out. What else was she to do? And what else was she to do but let him kiss her, hard and with tongue?

She cried about it afterward—after they took us home, after a terrifying hour (or maybe it was only ten minutes that felt like an hour) of being alone in her house with them. She cried and I told her it didn't have to count as her first boyfriend or her first kiss. Then we put on the angriest song we knew: "So What" by Metallica. Ironic considering it was all about the acts men can commit and shrug off including doing things to "a schoolgirl's twat." We chose it because it was loud and there was a lot of swearing. Because we wanted to say, *So fucking what?* to this night and forget it, though it was also already ingrained in us that society would say, *So fucking what?* about what had happened. "Boys will be boys" is just a euphemism for that, after all.

We didn't tell my friend's mom what happened, just played the insolent teenager card and said the boys were gross and we didn't want to see them again. I didn't tell my parents either. When I told another friend about it, she shrugged it off, saying that's just how boys were and I should get used it. That stung at the time. It made a lot more sense later when I found out that she'd been sexually abused as a child.

It did seem like nothing after that. And after I learned that another person I knew had been groped and pushed around daily by her guy friends when she was in sixth grade. And after another was raped by a relative in junior high. And after what happened to me sophomore year of high school.

But even though what happened to me that night at fourteen was common, was not as severe as what happened to my other friends or to me later, it still had an impact. I stopped playing pool with my male cousins in my aunt's basement. And more than a decade later, when a guy I really liked, the guy I would eventually marry, asked me on a date to play pool, I had a sinking sense of dread and shame. I didn't know how to explain why I didn't like to play.

Grab them by the pussy.

Just locker room talk.

Those phrases infiltrated my brain in October 2016. The violence behind the one. The dismissal, the devaluation of so many lived experiences, including my own, behind the other. The smug face that spoke them, the way he and so many others shrugged like those words didn't matter. This was the living, breathing embodiment of *So fucking what*. The embodiment of the years of damage endured by me and every other person who had had their body violated.

Perhaps because I had grown so used to being told in many ways that my body didn't matter—through boob grabs, through nonconsensual sex, through the many men trying to legislate what I could do with it—the first phrase didn't bother me as much as the second.

The second phrase gave permission; it created the space that made the first phrase possible. The second phrase is the justification behind rape culture. No, it simply *is* rape culture.

And it reminded me of my own locker room talk, which was a very different sort, but stemmed from that same idea that boys and men could say anything no matter whom it hurt.

The first place I went in my head when I heard that dismissal was not the pool hall or the back of that pickup truck. It was not the bedroom floor where the rug scraped against my bare ass and the ring on my necklace bruised my chest and tears bloomed in my eyes because I was too afraid to say stop. It was the locker room of my junior high. It was day after day after day in seventh and eighth grade, when I slumped down on the bench and pulled my regular clothes out of my locker, trying to change into them as quickly and discreetly as possible, not because I was modest but because I'd spent the last forty minutes being told by the boys in my class how ugly I was. My chest was flat as a board. My hair was stringy and gross. I looked like a man, not a girl.

So I didn't want to see my nonexistent breasts, my skinny legs that they said I should really learn to shave. I didn't want to look in the mirror and see the face or the body that was clearly freakish, ghoulish, and would never be loved.

That was my locker room talk. Their voices in my head, reducing me to the sum of my parts, and my parts were clearly worthless.

I was fifteen, a sophomore in high school, the first time I had sex. It seemed like most of my friends had already done it, but while that was in the back of my head, it was not the reason why I did it. Greg and I had been dating a month, and we were so deeply connected it felt like we'd always been together and always would be. Soul mates. True love. Like Kurt and Courtney. Like Sid and Nancy. Those were our versions of Romeo and Juliet, and we happily ignored the fact that they also ended in tragedy.

We did it for the first time in my bedroom. My parents were out, and I paid my little brother ten bucks to stay downstairs and watch TV. The entire act from when we started kissing until Greg was pulling off the condom lasted roughly twenty minutes or five and a half songs on an album I can no longer listen to. That album isn't banned from my life because of that night—I thought that night was blissful. I mean, the sex wasn't mind-blowing, but it wasn't painful like I'd feared it would be. It made me feel closer to Greg, as close as two people could get, and that was all I wanted. To feel like I wasn't that girl from the locker room anymore. I was not ugly and unloveable. My bond with Greg assured me of that.

We dated for almost six months. We had sex eighteen times. I'm not sure why I still remember that exact number. I do not at this point remember the proportions: how much of that was sex I wanted and how much was sex I endured because I thought I had to. I do remember the exact date that the switch occurred. Roughly three months into our relationship. April 11, 1995.

At that point I was down to one friend besides Greg; he'd found reasons for banishing all of the others from my life. My wardrobe had also been restricted: baggy band T-shirts and jeans were okay; the baby-doll dresses and fishnets I'd collected were not. He'd made me let him read my diary because nothing should be secret between us. I'd found a way of telling myself that all of these things were just signs that he cared, that we were so close, so in love. I found a way of swallowing my instincts, my gut feeling of wrongness. It would literally burn holes in my stomach; at sixteen I'd be diagnosed with ulcers.

April 11, 1995

It was raining. We were dropped off at the one remaining friend's house. Greg said that before going inside we should have sex in her garage. She was already right there at the window, and did I mention it was raining? So I said no, for the first and last time.

He gave me the silent treatment for hours until my friend convinced him to go into her bedroom with me and talk. Just talk. She was firm on that, and I was in agreement. I didn't want to have sex in her room. I didn't want to have sex at all.

But here's how the conversation went:

If you don't have sex with me, I feel rejected. We had sex before, so if you don't want to have it again, it must mean you don't love me. If you don't love me, we should break up. If we break up, I will die because you are the only person in the world that I care about. Are you rejecting me?

No.

Do you want to break up?

No.

Do you love me?

Yes. Of course, yes.

Saying yes to love meant saying yes to sex. And that is how I ended up on my friend's bedroom floor ("We can't use her bed" was my one caveat) with the rug scraping against my bare ass and the ring on my necklace bruising my chest and tears blooming in my eyes because I was too afraid to say, *Stop, this hurts,* because that might be perceived as rejection.

That is also how I repeatedly ended up on my knees in a park bathroom during lunch, ignoring the cold, the smell of piss, the ants marching by, and the grate of the drain digging into my skin.

That is also how I ended up in his basement having sex without a condom even though the thought of pregnancy terrified me.

The basement was the last time. He broke up with me after that because he wanted to have sex with other people.

Again, I don't know how many times out of that eighteen times total that I had sex with Greg out of fear instead of love or desire, but it was enough that sometimes I still freeze up during sex. Sometimes I'm still afraid to say no.

It was the Tuesday after "Grab them by the pussy" and "Just locker room talk," when I walked to the front of a university classroom and stated that I was a survivor. The woman standing next to me—my friend, colleague, and event co-organizer—stated that she was a survivor as well. We were there to read the words of another survivor, the woman whom Brock Turner, a nineteen-year-old freshman, had brutally assaulted on the Stanford campus in January of 2015. The woman, a twenty-two-year-old who'd attended a campus fraternity party with her sister, was intoxicated and unconscious when two international students found Turner on top of her behind a Dumpster. At the hearing and in the media, much was made of the fact that Turner was a swimmer with an athletic scholarship and how much *he* stood to lose if punished for, as his own father put it, "twenty minutes of action." The survivor read her powerful 7,138-word victim-impact statement at the sentencing, and after Turner received only six months despite this, her words were published online and read on the floor of the United States House of Representatives. Turner was released after serving only three months.

The highest number of sexual assaults on college campuses occur within the first six weeks of classes. We'd decided it was crucial to host a community reading of this survivor's letter and a discussion about rape culture during that window. It felt even more pressing after that weekend when rape culture had so brashly, *so unapologetically* been put on display.

Our campus is not huge and neither was our crowd—maybe thirty people who came and went over the two-hour period, but it was significant for every person who was there. The reading truly was a community reading. Everyone in that room was invited to come up when they felt so moved and read as much or as little as they wanted. A few lines, a page. "You can stop when it becomes too much," we told them. My friend and I started it off, we stepped in whenever there was not someone else up there to take a turn, and we both stood near the podium at all times so no one would be alone while reading.

I ended reading the last portion of the letter, where she thanks those who supported her—from her sister to the two men who saved her. I did so through thick tears because I'd forgotten to grab Kleenex from the box nearby. I choked up. I considered stepping back, but I didn't want to. I knew that the most powerful part was coming, where she addressed girls everywhere to say that she was with us, fighting alongside us, believing us, being a lighthouse and shining out in the darkness as a reminder that we are powerful, valuable, and cannot be silenced. I cleared my throat and let the words ring loud and true.

In that moment I was in two places at once. I was in a Seattle classroom in October of 2016 and I was in an anarchist space in

Chicago in May of 1996, at another event that I'd helped organize: The Midwest Girl Fest.

In the aftermath of my relationship with Greg, I'd taken
scalding-hot showers, I'd smashed mirrors and carved lines
and words like "Slut" and "Lost" with broken glass and sharp
pieces of metal, I'd starved myself just to prove I had control
over my own body, but I'd also found release in music. I'd
gravitated naturally to angry female voices. To Courtney Love
and Hole. To Kathleen Hanna and Bikini Kill. To Corin Tucker
and Heavens to Betsy, and later, Sleater-Kinney.

I immersed myself in their words, in their rage. I sought
more and more and through that I found a community of girls
who made music and zines and shouted for "Revolution Girl
Style Now!" Some still called themselves riot grrrls at that point,
though to others that movement had been flawed—and it was,
largely due to a lack of intersectionality—but they still wanted
to fight, to do something. So, those of us in Chicago birthed The
Midwest Girl Fest: a weekend of workshops and frank discussion about sexism, racism, and classism. There was also an open
mic, and though I had not been planning to read at it, I had a
journal with me. A journal containing a letter I'd written to Greg
about everything he'd done to me. I went up to that microphone
and read it through my tears, telling the full story of my relationship aloud for the very first time.

Girls I barely knew hugged me afterward. A lifelong friendship was sealed with the girl who held my hand as I spoke. The

open mic was recorded, and I made sure to get a copy. I listened to myself only a couple of times, but it was enough just to know that, like my musical heroines, I'd spoken my truth.

Strengthened by the response to my reading, I continued to write about my relationship with Greg. I put together zines about what I'd been through and I was grateful for the dialogue they created—for the girls I didn't even know who wrote me to say that sharing my experience gave them strength.

But it was easy for others to take the power I'd struggled to regain. In the last zine I ever made, just after I graduated high school, I'd included a handwritten, diary-style piece describing how "my boyfriend took me to a public bathroom at lunch to fuck me." Behind my handwriting, I'd collaged the typed words "rape" and "sexual assault." I also revealed that I'd cried about it for the first time just two days earlier and told my roommate, "I was raped, like, twice a week for a month."

It was the most vulnerable I'd ever been, not just speaking that word aloud, but putting it in print: rape. Before that I'd always said "sexual abuse" because I felt like I could defend my use of that phrase. I could say, "My boyfriend emotionally abused me and it led to sexual abuse." And in the same way I'd known deep down that what happened to my friend and me when we were fourteen would be easily dismissed, I'd also known that I *would* have to defend myself. That though no one in my life had taken Greg to task for his actions, my words would be put on trial. And sure enough they were.

After I mailed out my zine, a male friend sent me a letter telling me I was "victimizing" myself, and though I'm sure he used a euphemism of some sort, that I should get over it. He also made it clear that I didn't have the right to use words like "rape" or "sexual assault." Those were words for women who'd fought and said no.

For the next three years I drank heavily and wrote nothing, and those feelings of worthlessness, of being ugly and damaged only became more suffocating.

I was still struggling with how I was "allowed" to define my experience two decades later at that community reading of the Brock Turner survivor letter. After I finished reading, we opened the floor for discussion, a safe space to share. I didn't know if I was going to, but then a college student described her experience, which clearly, unquestionably was rape, and she followed it by saying, "But he was my boyfriend and we'd had sex before, so . . . I don't know what to call that."

I looked her in the eyes, mine tearing up again, and said, "I know exactly what you mean." Then I'd described how, a few months earlier, I'd seen a poster for an anti-rape campaign that read:

MYTH: "NO" MEANS "CONVINCE ME." IT'S NOT RAPE IF WE GET TO "YES."

FACT: COERCED SEX IS STILL RAPE, EVEN WITH THE LACK OF PHYSICAL FORCE, EVEN WITH A "YES."

"I was walking down the street and it was on a lamppost," I

told them. "I cried because a *lamppost* told me what I'd needed to hear since I was fifteen years old."

As it turned out, a few of the people there had seen that lamppost and also felt validated. I sent the picture I'd taken of it to them so we could always carry that with us: the knowledge that we believed one another and so did the strangers who'd made and put up those signs.

When the man who unapologetically committed sexual assault was elected as president of the United States, I felt like half of my country had betrayed me. Half of my country had said to me and every other survivor, *So fucking what?* It hurt deeply, but what bothered me the most is that, at my core, I'd expected it. There was a numb, cynical, conditioned part of me that had been there since before I was groped in that pool hall or harassed in gym class that knew I lived in a society that turned a blind eye to sexual violence in all of its forms.

No good has ever come from that numbness, though. I know that from the three years I wallowed in it after my experience had been invalidated and the words I used to define it were taken from me.

I know that speaking up is a matter of survival. And I am heartened by the fact that I see it happening more and more. That people are coming together on college campuses to tell their stories and talk about rape culture. That people are tweeting that they believe survivors, that they *are* survivors. That people are speaking out and saying unequivocally that "Grab them by the pussy" is sexual assault. That "Just locker room talk" is bullshit. It is rape culture. It is unacceptable.

There are people out there, I want to tell the version of me trying not to cry in a pool hall, on the bench of a gym locker room, on the dirty cement floor of a public bathroom, *people who will not say,* So fucking what? *They will not tell you how to define your experience. If you speak up, they will listen, and they will believe you, and together we can say,* These stories, these words, are mine.

Some days I find that I still can't speak up for me, but I can do it for the friends who were raped and abused at a young age. I can do it for the women and girls—cis and trans and genderqueer— all those people I've met only once, who bravely shared their stories in an anarchist space or in a college classroom. I can do it for everyone who has written me e-mails after hearing or reading my words to tell me their stories or just to say please keep speaking up because I don't feel like I can.

I can do it for you. For all of us. Our experiences matter. Our voices matter. And the deafening silence that protects those who have violated us must be broken.

FAT AND LOUD

Julie Murphy

Here's something that simply reading my printed words might not otherwise reveal: I'm fat. Not polite fat. Not Hollywood fat. Not cute fat. Not fat from certain angles. Not chubby. Or curvy. Or even voluptuous. Or some other euphemism for fat. No, I'm fat. Truly fat. And I always have been.

I'm also one of those angry feminists who won't shut the hell up. I'm that person at family dinners and events who is always bringing up politics. It almost never ends well, and yet I do it anyhow. I get into Facebook arguments as part of my nightly routine. I may not be changing minds in the comments section of my local newspaper's Facebook page, but if practice makes perfect, fighting in the comments section is my daily workout.

You might wonder what the hell my being fat has to do with my politics, but hear me out.

My tendency to always be political did not come out of the blue. It all started in second grade, when we had a classroom mock election to coincide with the 1992 election. Our choices were George H. W. Bush, Bill Clinton, and Ross Perot. I don't know what it was about that age, but I remember my world expanding that year. It was the first time I could remember being obsessed with the Olympics, too. It's not that my world was becoming bigger; it's that I was coming to realize that the world was and would always be big. It was me who would do the growing to meet my world, not the other way around.

Leading up to that Election Day in 1992, I spent many nights sitting with my dad as he watched the news. My dad was a life-long Democrat and encouraged me to vote for Bill Clinton. At that age, I'd do almost anything to make my dad proud, but I found myself obsessing over small details that had nothing to do with the candidates. Specifically Hillary Clinton's headbands and the texture and color of her hair.

I know. That's ridiculous. I wish I could say that I heard some sound bite of Hillary saying something profound, but I can't. What I can say is that six-year-old Julie was infatuated with headbands and Hillary Clinton seemed to be a fan, too. Not only that, but the color and texture of her hair appeared to be identical to my mother's hair, the same hair I'd spent hours running my stubby little fingers through. Neither of those are very good reasons to pledge devotion to someone, especially politically, but I do believe it was the reason that on the morning of my classroom's mock election I found myself voting for a Clinton. Just not the one on the ballot.

I'd like to say that one single moment turned me into the politically obsessed Thanksgiving-dinner-ruining monster that I am today, but I think that my love for politics was somehow more subtle, yet simultaneously fated, than that.

Because beneath all that is one enduring thing: my body. My fatness.

Before I move on, I should say: people often cringe when I use the word "fat." Please understand that when I say I'm fat, I'm not insulting or demeaning myself, but am instead merely using the word as a descriptor. I love my body and am thankful for all the ways it serves me. Me calling my body fat is no different from saying someone else is tall or freckled. Or that Hillary Clinton has blond hair!

That said, we live in a world where very clear messages have been sent about the kinds of bodies that we are allowed to have. I can barely even check my e-mail in the morning without seeing a thin, white woman on the Internet telling me how I should look and live and strive to be. I can't look through the popular search page on Instagram without seeing what my #bodygoals should be, and Pinterest is just a breeding ground for thigh-gap obsessions. But my body has never been what is considered acceptable.

In high school, I was never a very good student or much of a reader, but I was definitely fat and I was also a total theater kid. 100 percent show trash. Whether I was doing tech on a show, stage-managing, rounding out the chorus, or playing a leading role, you could find me with either my high school theater crew or backstage at one of my local community theaters. The theater world was a safe haven for me to come to terms with my body in a really honest way and to also make connections with other people who felt like they didn't quite fit for whatever reason.

But few things are ever exclusively good or exclusively bad, so theater came with its own issues. My main beef, however, was this: fat girls are almost exclusively cast in one of two roles, which meant my options were either the maternal figure or the unruly homeless woman. And this was fine . . . for a while. But by my senior year, I was exasperated with my limited options and had pretty much resigned myself to only doing costumes for shows, because when I did get a big role with some serious lines or even my own song, I had most definitely been cast as one of those two archetypes.

I didn't pick up writing until much later, and now looking back, it all makes sense that this is where I've ultimately ended—creating my own stories. But at the time I was tired of being everyone else's supporting cast in everyone else's shows, when in real life I had always been the main character of my own story. What was even more difficult for me to understand was that my high school drama teacher was a fat woman and always had been. If anyone knew how much it sucked to never be the girl in a show who gets to fall in love or go on an adventure, it was her.

It all came crashing down for me when my high school put on the play that my drama teacher had written herself. I won't lie; it was totally cheesy and self-indulgent on her part, but when it comes to the spotlight, High School Julie was like a cat in a patch of sunlight—totally and blissfully relaxed. If there were ever a play where I could win the role of the leading lady, this would be it. I mean, my teacher—a fellow fatty!—wrote the damn thing. There was no predetermined standard here like there were with other shows like *Annie* or *The Sound of Music*. This was my moment. I was sure of it.

To be honest, in my real life, I always did everything I could to buck against the stereotypes of the fat girl. That was for lots of different reasons—some of them really good and some of them really bad. But for the purpose of this essay, you should know that I had all kinds of friends and had gone on dates and adventures. The life I'd lived thus far did not reflect any fictional fat girl I had ever come across. So I knew from firsthand experience that the fat experience could be so much more than the aging matriarch or the panhandling woman on the corner.

But my fat drama teacher, who had lived so much of my struggle and more, cast me as the grandmother—the only woman onstage whom the audience could possibly forgive for being fat because she already had one foot in the grave anyway.

I took the role. And I cried. I cried for a whole weekend, and then after the show was over, I stopped auditioning for school plays and musicals. And then eventually I stopped auditioning for anything at all.

It took me a while to find my way back to the arts—in the form of writing—but when I did, I knew one thing for sure: after years of crash dieting all through high school and college, I wasn't changing for the world. The world would have to change for me.

Over the years I've discovered there's something about fat bodies that really pisses people off. That anger manifests itself in many ways. Sometimes it's a silent sneer. Sometimes it's a comment on the Internet. Sometimes it's things that don't even feel like anger at first. Like when I'm eating a salad—because, SURPRISE, fat people can enjoy "healthy" food—and someone tells me what a good job I'm doing or how proud they are of me. Or when someone tells me how brave I am to love myself or to wear a swimsuit in public. (Because how dare I have the audacity, right?) But every once in a while it really is someone acting as a plain old-fashioned bully. Like when I'm on a plane and some jerk says just loud enough for me to hear that he hopes he won't be so misfortunate as to have to sit next to me.

When I really think back to the why and how of what got me so political in the first place, it always comes back to this: my fat body gave me no choice in the matter. The reason why society— men especially—are so easily upset by fatness is because it's a giant (no pun intended!) middle finger to every dude who thinks that the female body exists for nothing less than the male gaze (or dude eye candy if you're not familiar with that phrase). It's a blatant and unapologetic reminder that female bodies do not exist for the sole purpose of male pleasure.

Something about being fat made me loud. I think there are a couple different tendencies when you're fat—some days we wake up and think we can conquer the world, and other days we feel like the "before" picture from a weight loss commercial. But most often my tendency is to be loud. Not loud in an obnoxious way, but in a way that guarantees I'm heard. Sometimes I'm loud out of anger or passion or even just self-preservation. Regardless of my motivation, I gathered pretty early on in life that people were looking at me, and so I decided that if they were looking at me, I might as well make them listen, too.

The problem is I'm still figuring out what I want to say. I'm still learning all the ways the color of my skin gives me privilege and how that privilege will always overrule the other parts of myself, like the size of my body or my bisexuality, that might define me as other. I'm learning that acknowledging my privilege as a white lady means understanding that just because something is not a problem for me does not mean it is not a problem. I know that the best way for me to use my privilege is to examine the ways it intersects with someone else's oppression. So when I get loud about being fat, I am sure to make room for women to be loud about being fat and Black or Asian or Muslim or whatever other thing makes them different. And sometimes being loud means knowing when to be quiet. Sometimes it means sitting back and listening to the experiences and needs of others around you.

I think that in every person's life there is a pivotal world moment that defines before and after. For a lot of people I know, that moment was 9/11, or for others the war in Iraq. For my dad it was the Nixon administration. For my mom it was Woodstock. (Yes, my mom was at Woodstock. Yes, the stories are amazing.) And for me I think that moment will always be the 2016 election. The results of that election forced me to closely examine my life up until that point and to also decide how I would move through the world from that moment on.

I'm a pessimist by choice. Choosing to always expect the worst-case scenario protects me in many ways. I'm a prickly grouch who cares too much about almost everything and cries out of anger and explodes inside any time someone tries to comfort me. So trust me when I say it's always best if I'm prepared for the worst.

But the 2016 election defied all logic for me. Donald Trump was too outrageous—too orange!—to ever be a real contender. And he was running against Hillary! Headband-wearing Hillary, who is by no means perfect but felt like the type of person who always turned in her homework early and didn't even need to use the book during an open-book test. Those sound like ideal presidential qualities if you ask me, but maybe smart women make people uncomfortable for the same reason fat ladies do.

I was shocked on November 8, 2016. (Which unfortunately also happened to be my thirty-first birthday. Boo.) I barely slept for days. I dreaded traveling for work that weekend. I felt betrayed by this country—a country I loved despite her many flaws. Suddenly America was an ugly place.

Except that nothing about America's ugliness was sudden. The only sudden thing about it was my realization.

Here is my truth: I am a fat, white, bisexual, cis lady in a hetero relationship. I'd always thought parts of my identity demanded that I be political, that I had no choice. And to an extent that was true. My fatness made me loud. Like many others, I spent the months leading up to the election being very loud. But I wasn't listening. I wasn't hearing when friends of color told me that Trump was nominated for a reason. Enough Americans believed in his vision of America for that to be the case. I wasn't listening when people said that white women were choosing their race over their sex in the ballot box. I wasn't listening.

In the weeks after the election, liberals everywhere took turns pointing fingers at one another, searching for the root cause of this catastrophe. I took a few days to be sad and mourn the fact that HRC, my headband-wearing problematic fave, will most likely never see her dream come true. I licked my wounds, but not for long. Instead I've spent most my post-2016-Election-Day time calling my representatives and being more active than ever before, because if this is the reality many Americans have always lived with, then my ignorance has made me complicit. Most of all, though, I'm listening. I'm making room for voices that aren't always white or cis or hetero. Because my resistance is intersectional or it is not at all.

Since the election and as of the writing of this essay, there have been lots of protests happening across the country and in return lots of media coverage. And because fat jokes are low-hanging fruit, there have been endless comments from media outlets, pundits, and even lawmakers about how Trump got more fat women walking in one day (the day of the Women's March) than Michelle Obama did in eight years. (Side note: The first lady is always put in charge of the "war on obesity." That nonsense is another essay for another day.)

When I saw those jokes crop up, I sighed. Business as usual. Fat ladies. We're used to being the butt of the joke. Then I thought back to what had made me such a political person to begin with. My body. My fat body. My big fat middle finger to the patriarchy. And I could not have been prouder.

Things are happening. Conversations are turning into action. We, as a country, are being forced to look at our own reflection in a way many of us never have before. It's uncomfortable and it hurts. And if some dumbass people on the Internet want to say that a whole bunch of fat ladies led the charge, well, then count me among them.

MYTH MAKING: IN THE WAKE OF HARDSHIP

Somaiya Daud

When I was six, my sister and I got into an argument about what (who?) we were. I can't remember which sides of the argument we fell on but that the options seemed to be Black or Arab (we're not Arab). In an effort to have it decided once and for all, we turned to our father. His response has stuck with me my entire life: "Those things don't matter," he said. "You're Muslim."

Identity is a tricky thing when it's something that matters, when your conception of self is built around it, whether it's hidden or slapped onto your skin for people to comment on and react to. When I was a child, I wanted the easy answer—I am this or this, not both, and certainly not three things; categories aren't messy; history is a straightforward narrative arc with no steps back or sideways; how you look and act matches who you are or who people expect you to be. But the older I got, the more the lines blurred, the more I realized there's not really a hierarchy of identity but a strange constellation within myself. Some stars shone brighter than others depending on where I was or who I was with, and some are pole stars and no matter what happens, they don't change.

"Writer" is not an identity, or rather, not an identity in the ways that "Black," "Moroccan," and "Muslim" are. But it's always been a deeply embedded part of me, impossible to separate from the ways I see the world and engage with it. I wrote a collection of alliterative poetry in the fourth grade and never really looked back.[1] After that I wrote wherever I was, no matter the circumstance. I sketched out stories for my kid cousins, wrote poetry (of the angsty lovesick variety) all through high school, experimented with most forms of prose (short story, novella, fan fiction), and in my senior year of high school started a novel I never finished. When people ask me what I write now, I say, "Spec fic. *Only.*" As a high schooler I wasn't so rigid. I wrote contemporary short stories in verse, fantasy, and science fiction, and there was a short six-month window when I tried to be a graphic artist.[2]

When my mother realized I was writing, she was ecstatic.

---

1. I realize this sounds incredibly fancy. That's because it *was*. It had a fabric jacket!
2. Not being immediately excellent at this, I quit.

Above all she wanted me to be a doctor (and in that, I only half disappointed; being a doctor of philosophy is better than not being a doctor at all), but her family had a strong literary tradition. When I was eighteen she asked me why I hadn't tried to get anything I'd written published. By then I was a "Writer," capital W. When people said "Oh, you're a writer?" I'd beam and say, "Yes! I'm working on my novel right now. So if you'll excuse me . . ."

Being a Writer was uncomplicated in a way my other identities were not. No one ever looked me up and down and said, "Wow, you don't *look* like a writer," the way they did when I said I was Black or Moroccan. No one ever squinted at me and said, "Quick, speak a fantasy language," the way they asked me to speak Arabic on command like a parrot. And no one ever looked at me sideways, hummed thoughtfully, and said, "You look more like a painter to me," as they did when slyly suggesting I was lying about my heritage.

When I was in the fifth grade my teacher gave me a copy of *The Hobbit*. I don't know that I'd read very much fantasy by then. My dad had fed me on a steady diet of *Star Wars* (which, until Ewan McGregor, had given me nightmares of Jabba the Hutt eating me), and I think I read *The Lion, the Witch, and the Wardrobe* the same year. But *The Hobbit* was my first introduction to high fantasy. I dove in and never looked back: elves, goblins, magic, dangerous and dark forests; after a while I didn't want to read anything else. All the non-fantasy reading I'd done fell to the wayside in favor of places that didn't exist and creatures that lurked in my imagination.

From there it was only a short hop and skip to *writing* fantasy. In the real world I had to wrestle with how people saw me, but in my fake Tolkien worlds (because that's what they were, no matter how much eleven-year-old me bristles) there were no such demands. Categories were easy, history was fluid, and every character was who they were because I said so.

I grew up in a community that was predominately populated by immigrants. It was a weird mix between college town (literally called College Park) and suburb. The local Muslim community bought some property and turned it into a mosque-slash-school, which I attended through sixth grade. I didn't realize how lucky I was that I grew up and went to school with people who looked like me, worshipped as I did, and had the same third-culture problems. And I didn't know until I was an adult how much work went into a community like that. We didn't just have a school and a place of worship. There was a small indie publisher that published picture books, books for young readers, and young adult books. I grew up hearing Arabic, Hindi, Urdu, English, and Pashto. I was never the Weird Muslim Girl because we were all Muslim girls.

I say all that to frame how I read. For the most part, it wasn't a huge leap for me to envision the characters I read as people who looked like me or my friends. Most books' physical descriptions are vague, and even those that weren't never felt binding. I can't say with any firmness if I *believed* all the characters were people of color, or if I did the extra mental work knowing that they weren't. But either way it would be dishonest to say that I felt like a cultural vampire during my childhood. (Boy would that *change*.)

Then, of course, came Tolkien. There's a lot to be said *for* Tolkien. He rescued *Beowulf* from obscurity. He's a master world crafter, and the number of materials published posthumously are a testament to that. The world he created was a lifelong project, and the depth and breadth of it *shows*. Despite reading more like nonfiction than a novel, *The Silmarillion* is still deeply compelling and moving. But the inherent racism of that world is really difficult to miss. From orcs and goblins to the ways that "men of the east" are assigned to evil, even eleven-year-old me *noticed*. Everything beautiful, everything I loved about the world of Arda, the world *The Lord of the Rings* takes place in, belonged to people aggressively coded as not like me. The few women there were all fair skinned, often fair haired, and light eyed. One of them literally has the appellation "the White." The whiteness of Tolkien's world wasn't just in the way he populated it, but deeply embedded in its language and signs. Heaven is "the True West," the *sound* of the Free Peoples of Middle-earth is the horn, while orcs and goblins are heralded by drums,[1] and so on.

---

1. Horns are, in the Western literary tradition, usually coded as white. They're used to signal and herald the arrival of kings and heroes. Drums, on the other hand, were used by Muslims during war. The North African Almohads famously used drums and poetry to intimidate their enemies on the battlefield, something Tolkien was likely familiar with, if not in that specific capacity, then generally.

A nice way of describing my personality is contrarian. If you tell me something isn't for me or that I'm not allowed or that the door is closed, I will dig my heels in. I'll break down the door or lose my voice yelling about how that is absolutely my space and also fuck you. So it's no surprise that I waded into Tolkien, got the message that *I Was Not Welcome,* and then took over the house despite the huge YOU'RE NOT WELCOME sign in the window. The bones and foundation were good, I said to myself. The decoration was shit. I'd have to tear down the wallpaper and all the portraits in the main hall, and then put up my own stuff to make it mine. I also wanted to call up the ghost of Tolkien and let him know, in case he didn't, that making your elves all look the same and then dividing them up based on arbitrary categories was not actually diversity. Assuming he cared. I'd bet he didn't.

I began writing my first fantasy project when I was twelve. I kept it in a red spiral notebook, now thankfully lost. I remember it way too clearly, though: it was set in the elvish refuge Lothlórien, and featured a brown-skinned elvish princess. The opening scene was her standing in front of a crystalline pool, crying as she realized the elf she loved didn't love her back. He'd insinuated himself into her good graces in the name of securing her crystal jewel. The crystal jewel was probably a fake ring of power. What's important here is *not* that I thought I was writing original fiction (oh, to be so young again), but that the elvish princess was brown.

It seemed both natural and necessary that the characters I

wrote were brown, even if the worlds I was stealing from were not. I'd grown up surrounded by people who looked like me, who told me that my stories were necessary and valued, and who worked actively against the very loud media narrative that I was strange or didn't belong. Eleven-year-old me didn't recognize that simple act for what it was: a necessary and powerful resistance to a literary tradition deeply invested in keeping people like me out.

The world of my imagination was my respite in a world that was becoming overtly hostile. The same year I wrote my Tolkien fan fiction the two towers at the World Trade Center collapsed after a pair of planes were deliberately crashed into them and a third plane was crashed into the Pentagon (less than twenty minutes from where I lived). Islamophobia wasn't invented with the terrorist attacks in 2001, but it felt to me as if the safe and easy world I'd known dissolved away in a single instant. The mirror my parents held up for me was gone, and what I had in its place was the increasingly ham-fisted allegories in the media for East/West geopolitical relations and the small worlds I created in my mind.

The week after 9/11 the Islamic school I attended and the mosque attached to it were closed. Someone stuck and burned a cross on the lawn. A few months later a story circulated about a Muslim woman at a stoplight who was pulled from her car by her hijab and beaten. After a while it became really clear—if you were Muslim or *looked* Muslim you were a target, and there were rarely people who were willing to step in and put a stop to it.

In 2003 I sat with my mother and sisters in my living room and watched the televised broadcast of the first bombing of Baghdad in what would come to be called the Iraq War. As much as Bush claimed this was part of the War on Terror and not an international expression of how everyone felt about Muslims, it definitely *felt* like the latter.

Despite not being the direct victim of hate crimes, it was hard not to notice the looks when I went out with my family, especially after I started wearing hijab. Walking through life felt like being a clenched fist all of a sudden. I was always waiting for the ax to drop, for someone to step too close or cross from firm into hostile. It was exhausting to walk out of my house every day and wait for the bus afraid, walk home afraid, go to the grocery store afraid.

And then, of course, I switched schools. We moved in 2005, and so I said good-bye to my middle school friends and the safe environment of an Islamic school. Gone were the familiar faces, and the familiar dress, and the familiar languages. Granted, the school I transferred to wasn't an all-white space, but it wasn't the same and it presented a new set of challenges and fears. Up until then, I'd never thought of myself as a shy person. But I was terrified of this new environment, and the loud overbearing girl I'd been disappeared.

The more shy I became, the more I retreated into reading

and writing. Here were worlds I could control, problems I could solve, characters I knew and understood. There was something familiar and reassuring in crafting new worlds with problems both extraordinary and similar to mine. Made suddenly bold in my writing, I tried my hands at a novel.

I never finished it.

I was nineteen when I finished writing my first book. It was the first year I'd participated in NaNoWriMo and *won*, and I don't think there was anyone prouder except for my mother. Now that I'd managed to write one book, I knew I could write another and another and another. Writing a novel was no longer an elusive and magical skill, given to only a few. I had it! I'd done it through sheer perseverance during my first year of college, through all its ups and downs.

Thinking back on that first novel (I no longer have it, thank you, short life span of the PC), I have to laugh a little. A friend gave me some well-meaning, but ultimately incorrect, advice: the average young adult novel was anywhere between one hundred and one hundred and twenty thousand words. My first novel was one hundred and *fifty* thousand words long, really three books smashed into one. It was neither high fantasy nor science fiction, so the length was entirely unjustified.

More importantly: it was bad.

I can't remember what my prose was like (probably also bad), but when I was nineteen I didn't understand how to write a story. Stories have arcs, rising action, falling action, climaxes, and denouement. A good book can control its pacing, can keep the reader invested even when it slows a little. It took me a long time to understand that books were not supposed to imitate *life*. They reflect the real world in important ways, but the phrase "truth is stranger than fiction" exists for a reason. In fiction, coincidence is rare, and most things are causal. Everything *should* serve a purpose because the best narratives are built consciously and with great deliberation.[1]

I didn't know any of these things. I only knew what I felt compelled to write. The overlarge story of a girl who fit in neither at school nor at home. Who feared being turned away by strangers as much as she feared being turned away by people who loved her. Who was eventually hunted down and spent a greater part of her adolescence looking over her shoulder. She gave up on normalcy, on being able to not run, on peace. I remember many things about this character—who I named Behzad—most of them fond. But the two things I remember the most are her feelings of being pursued relentlessly and her ability to come back to life once killed.

I was a macabre teen—I think many would likely argue I'm an equally macabre adult. In the first scene where her immortality

---

1. This is why your tenth-grade English teacher is asking you why the curtains are pink. Often pink curtains are just pink curtains—but the author put them there for a reason. Because the room needed pink curtains or because the pink curtains are Symbols. With a capital *S*.

is revealed, she is shot point-blank between the eyes. When she wakes up her face is covered in the blood and gore of her former body. It's hard, for me at least, to not draw the parallels between this scene and my teenage self's question of *why?* Why did we have to keep going on? Why, when we were hated and pursued and put on lists, did we have to get up every morning and go out and face the day? Behzad was a girl filled with bitterness and anger, and a large part of it was turned inward at her inability to simply die and be done with it. Her genetics *forced her* to get up every single day.

The narratives we build around and about ourselves and our communities are rarely rooted in truth. By that I don't mean that there *is* an inner truth from which one can build, but that as in most things in life, there is *no narrative.* Fantasy, and fiction in general, is compelling because it rationalizes the bizarre and the strange. Earth, life, the *self* bangs along, out of sync, doing as it likes and oftentimes without discernible order or logic. We tell stories to make sense of that—the weird, the ugly, the sudden and terrifying. We want to say, *great character arc, self,* but the truth is just as many people stall out in their nascent stages as people who veer wildly off course in ways we'd never believe if put down in a novel.

Seventeen-year-old Somaiya was certainly not forced to get up every day and face a world that seemed to hate her, but it often felt that way. What was I supposed to do? How was I supposed to navigate my life, when faced with so much hate? Behzad's answer to that question was *fight, live, survive.*

* * *

When Morocco secured its independence in 1956, it faced a "problem"—it was a new country with new borders (historically, the Maghreb stretched from the west coast of modern-day Morocco over most of North Africa), with a population of diverse ethnic groups (collectively called Amazigh) who were (and are) fiercely loyal to and proud of their heritages. In a violent effort to show an outward-facing unified identity, the government imposed a regime of Arabization. Most Moroccans already spoke Arabic, but under the new laws, indigenous languages weren't taught in schools, weren't used on signage, and indigenous names could not be put on birth certificates.[1]

I am not Arab. But I grew up in a community where the identities that were readily accepted or took precedence were Muslim, Black, the daughter of an immigrant. The messiness and complexity of identity (mine and others) were flattened and neatened so that other, more pressing conversations and solidarity movements could take place. It was more important that I spoke Arabic (as did all the students at my Islamic school), more important that my mother immigrated here before I was born, more important that I carried around the strange, bittersweet nostalgia for a motherland I'd never seen.

I knew that I was Amazigh. My grandmother and eldest aunt

---

1. This is changing, however slowly, thanks to groups of activists in Morocco and across North Africa who are fighting and lobbying for the right to indigenous cultural expression (among many other things).

both wore Amazigh facial tattoos specific to our Schlouh ethnic group, and many of my cousins spoke Teschelhit. And yet, somehow, through most of my life I carried the Arab and Amazigh identity inside me, side by side. It never felt as if they were in tension with each other, or that they struggled over and against each other. Perhaps because I didn't speak Teschelhit, and perhaps because the myth of an Arab Moroccan culture is exactly that, the part of me that could speak Arabic and the part that saw my grandmother's facial tattoos spoke to and fed each other.

It was a strange thing, then, to begin to come into the knowledge of the violence of taking on the Arab label while also being confronted with other frustrating myths. I am Black and Amazigh and Muslim, and yet to hear it from other people, I am none of those things. I don't code Black enough for some, and for others I'm Muslim so I must be Arab. Because I must be Arab, I am then a colonizer, with no claim to my mother's homeland and no right to her cultural legacy. I am an interloper, a liar, a deceiver, a thief. And, of course, to others I am worse things. You just have to turn on the news to see.

Like I said, identities are messy. They always overflow the boundaries we set up. The ways we nurture them and the ways people assail or erect false limits shape the people we become. It becomes easy to hide, or to run, or to scream, or to fight, depending on whether you've been dammed up or told to reroute for safety. I fall somewhere in between. I know who and what I am, and people who are wrong about those things don't matter. I am still an intersection of identities, sometimes in tension and sometimes in harmony. *That* is immovable and unchangeable, whether someone chooses to believe me or not.

So we return once again to eleven-year-old me writing her brown elvish princess. Writing myself into fantasy was just as much about imposing a narrative structure on my identity and on people's reception to it as it was about engaging my writer's identity with my racial and religious one. I sought out fantasy—to read and to write—because it felt and still feels aspirational to me. At its best, it's about fashioning a mythic space that gives us the room to imagine what sorts of greatness we can achieve. That greatness is often metaphoric (though I wouldn't say no to being a witch-queen), but it's a cultural and personal imaginary space where we can achieve greatness against all odds. For a girl living in a reality where her very existence is threatened, this mythology, this *possibility,* is crucial and necessary. And making space for myself, *carving* that space out, Tolkien's ghost be damned, is just as much about the narrative necessity to create those myths as it is about how much fun I have.

I rewatched *The Return of the King* recently, and then immediately after read Tolkien's tragedy *The Children of Húrin.* I was surprised to find that I disliked *ROTK* this time. *The Two Towers* has always been my favorite of the trilogy; in terms of character work and narrative drive and the pacing (despite the seeming never-endingness of Helm's Deep). I've loved this world since the fifth grade, and loved the Elves most of all, and so when I came away from this latest rewatch feeling sad and almost discouraged I was confused.

This time something of Tolkien's project with Arda revealed itself to me, and it was a project that I fundamentally disliked. The waning of the Elves and the dominion of Men and the static comfort of the Shire were all things I understood and still understand in their way. But I realized this time that *The Lord of the Rings* trilogy is about the closing of an age in Arda and the inability of Middle-earth to ever replicate it. Aragorn will remind people of the kings of old, but he is the last reminder. There will be no more great kings of Gondor; there will be no great alliances between Men and Elves. The age of heroes is past, and the age of something quieter and less grand and pale in comparison has begun.

It's nostalgia to the nth degree, but with a nihilistic bend. And in the context of the aftermath of the First World War, it makes sense. As a tool of imperialism, it's a compelling narrative, one that drives a person to seek that glory again and again. But if you're on the losing side of imperialism, it kind of blows. Your glory days didn't pass in some great victory. You did not triumph over evil. You lost, and your loved ones are gone, your holy places are toppled or ransacked, your tombs and cemeteries looted, and on and on.

This is not a myth I am interested in. I am deeply suspicious of nostalgia, even as I recognize what a powerful tool it is for the downtrodden. But the myth of never again reaching our former glories, of never again being great, is anathema to my whole person. Empires die; that's the way of things. But we're not dead. We didn't pass into history books with great places bombed out by however many wars. We are decolonized or decolonizing, and greatness may look different now. We are in diaspora, or we cannot trace our way home, or we do not recognize that place as home. But there are other ways to build greatness, other ways to shine brilliantly, to be glorious and luminary. Those things have not gone into the past. We will have to remake what they mean, we will have to define a future that does not rely fully on what we were and will instead have to imagine what we can become. And there is power in that myth making, in recognizing that we live and that there is something precious in that living, that we can pass that down to someone else, that we can lay down a new path for a different future, that we can *write it* out from under the shadow of whatever glorious structure or moment we hold dear to our hearts that has passed into the annals of history.

CHANGING CONSTELLATIONS

Nina LaCour

The town I grew up in was beautiful, but I didn't want to be there. Nestled within the San Francisco Bay Area, it was a valley surrounded by hills—green or golden depending on the season—with no train station or freeway exit. In order to get in or out you had to go through somewhere else. I felt trapped there, suspended.

I remember the early-morning suburban sky. The glow of the 7-Eleven behind the bus stop where I waited each morning with my best friend, Amanda. On the good mornings, when we woke early and felt like walking, we'd meet inside the store to get hot chocolates before setting out—first through the strip mall with its still-quiet stores, and then on a trail behind the new condominiums and houses. Eventually it would spill us out onto the far side of campus, whether we were ready or not. I was never ready. On that trail with my friend, I was at home in a town that rarely felt like home to me.

Amanda and I were among the few apartment kids in town. Everyone else had money. Everyone drove expensive cars to school. I remember being called as a junior to the college counselor's office, where I explained that I was only applying to state colleges because I would be paying my way through school. The counselor was so puzzled by the idea that she set down her pen, squinted her eyes at me, and asked if I was an emancipated minor.

I was filled with an anxiety around being wrong, around not understanding. From third grade on, math class paralyzed me; I still have nightmares about it. I wanted to talk in English class about books and poems but lacked the courage to raise my hand.

It was a community of clubs and teams. The country club. The Boy Scouts and Girl Scouts. Swim team and soccer and cross-country. Football and volleyball and baseball and cheerleading and basketball. Choir and band. I was part of none of it. "You weren't ever much of a joiner," my dad says now, reflecting. But I don't think it was so simple. I always felt as though I was on the periphery; I didn't know the way into anything. Part of me wanted to stand out, to be admired as different. I took guitar lessons and wrote poetry and loved being onstage in drama—but the louder part of me, the part so afraid of getting things wrong, told myself that the best I could hope for was to get through four years unnoticed.

Our freshman year, Amanda and I had French class first period. We were already inseparable, passing notes instead of focusing on our elderly teacher's lectures. Her glasses magnified her eyes as she glared at us, hawklike, whenever we were late, asking if we had gotten lost at the mall. If any of us did something to distress her, she would tell us, "Go play on the freeway." The boy sitting next to me sneered and rolled his eyes at the ridiculousness of it all. And then, one day, he passed me a note. I don't remember what it said, but I imagine that it was wry and funny and probably a little mean.

Soon the three of us were passing notes together, wondering if our teacher was really as bizarre as she presented herself to be or if it was all an act. What motive could she possibly have to maintain this ruse? *To strike fear in us,* Amanda and I said. *No, no,* Billy said. *To keep herself entertained through decades of teaching basic vocabulary and grammar to obnoxious teenagers like us.* Billy had art with me too, but where he enjoyed our French teacher's quirks, he loathed our art teacher's rigidity. The only good part of Art One, according to Billy, was that we could listen to music as we drew. At the time I listened almost exclusively to rap, which he loathed, so he set out to change my musical tastes, one mixtape at a time.

It didn't take long for me to realize that most of the artists on the mixes he made me were queer, and I wondered if I was supposed to understand that he was too. I would have assumed he was gay even without the mixes, but he'd never mentioned anything either way. I figured he'd let me know eventually.

Then one day he arrived to school effervescent with excitement. He'd seen a musician named Ani DiFranco play in the Berkeley High gym that weekend and now I needed to hear her. He clutched a tape to his heart and then placed it into my hands. He explained that he'd meant this to be another mix with many artists, but once he started choosing songs by her he couldn't stop. He was sure I was going to love her so much that I'd forget all about Tupac and Wu-Tang Clan.

Ceremoniously, Billy removed my Walkman from my backpack and clicked the tape in. He placed the headphones over my ears.

"You're going to love this," he said, pressing play. "It's going to change your life."

The first song was "Untouchable Face." It started slowly, a pattern of notes from an electric guitar, simple lines sung at a brokenhearted whisper. And then the chorus began with a passionate "Fuck you," so full of longing, so surprising coming from this sweet girl voice. I didn't know how to be angry or messy in the way she was. I listened to her in amazement, wondering, for the first time, if my life would one day open up into one as complicated and vital and real as hers.

Billy had a secret to tell me. He pressed nervously handwritten notes into my palm for weeks, stating only that.

"So tell me!" I'd say.

"I can't!" he'd wail, hands covering his face.

I didn't know why it was so difficult for him. All we talked about now was Ani DiFranco. If there had existed any question that I was homophobic, our mutual infatuation with this bisexual punk/folk singer should have reassured him otherwise. But he was so nervous that for the day or two before he told me I found myself worrying that I had perhaps read him entirely wrong. Maybe he was trying to tell me that he *liked* me. That kind of secret would have been a problem; my romantic attention was entirely consumed by a senior who would end up being my boyfriend for almost four years.

But no, he was gay. His palms were sweaty, his face bright red. He was smiling, but he looked like he might cry.

"Yeah," I said. "I mean, I figured."

"You *did*?" He dropped his jaw.

I smiled and shrugged. He'd made me mixes composed of Rufus Wainwright and the Indigo Girls, yet he thought I'd be surprised. He came out to his parents next, to mixed reactions, and finally, slowly, to the rest of the school. There was a group of older girls who took him in and helped him start a GSA. It was the first and only club I ever joined in all my years of school, but it was also short-lived and disorganized, and Billy's growing cynicism obstructed the older girls' goals of increasing attendance. He was the only openly queer kid in the school. I could see how the club was weighing on him.

Even though this was the San Francisco Bay Area in the late nineties, once the word spread, Billy got slammed into walls.

He got hate notes slipped through the vents of his locker. The girls graduated and the next year was worse than the first. When I saw the bruises and he told me who had given them to him, I had trouble believing it. These were boys I thought were funny, even nice. Once I saw the end of an assault from the far entrance of a hallway. The boys headed away as though nothing had happened while Billy pounded his locker with his fist before picking his textbooks up off the ground. I remember he was crying.

I remember not knowing what to do, and then doing nothing. At night, in my quiet room, I imagined myself a different girl, a braver one. One who knew the right words and how to use them, who would have hurled a perfect insult, who would have made Billy feel protected. This version of me would not have cared that the guys were nice most of the time. She would have held them accountable for their cruelty.

Maybe in the future I would be this way. Not so silent. Not so confused.

I practiced speaking up in my government class. We were nearing an election, and on the California ballot were a number of propositions that I knew in my heart were ethically wrong—one attempting to try minors as adults and another restricting marriage to that between one man and one woman. (Same-sex marriage was already not allowed; this proposition was to make it *extra* not allowed.) I can still see the seating arrangement and the faces of my classmates and feel how difficult it was for me every time I raised my hand and made an argument. Some of my classmates saw the discussions as purely philosophical, but every time I spoke my voice shook and I was close to tears. These were *people* we were talking about. Real *lives*. I was making myself heard for the first time in my life, but it wasn't enough, and I knew it. Billy still had bruises. I still smiled back at the boys who shoved Billy into walls when they smiled at me.

Billy still wrote me notes, but now they were long revenge fantasies about our classmates and the teachers who either turned a blind eye or joined in his ridicule.

As time passed he adopted a tough style. He practiced a hard gaze and an aloof posture. None of it worked. Eventually, he dropped out and finished high school by way of independent study through the continuation school.

I missed him often, but especially in French, when I thought of how he'd use our latest vocabulary words to ponder whether or not our teacher was a con artist or just severely jaded, his expressions animated, his accent graceful and precise.

And I was struck by the injustice of it. Our school boasted 100 percent graduation rates and nearly as many students feeding straight into four-year colleges. But it's easy to graduate students and send them to college when they're Eagle Scouts or soccer stars. I stayed awake at night thinking about it. Each time our principal walked past me in the hallways smiling, I fumed, knowing he didn't actually care about the students who needed him. Amanda and I discussed the hypocrisy of it on our walks to school. Billy was so smart and so worthy of support, and yet he was so easy for them to let go.

Billy and I kept in touch, talking on the phone at night in our respective bedrooms. Sometimes he came over and had dinner with my family. More often we met up at the café one town over.

In my family, we didn't express anger. That feeling was an underground stream, so silent and invisible I forgot it existed. If anger appeared at all, it was in a flicker of an expression: tight lips, furrowed brows. A retreat to a bedroom, a door shutting until the feeling was contained and we emerged smiling, ready to get on with our lives.

Billy wore his anger in smudges of black eyeliner and coats of black nail polish and drugstore black hair dye to cover his blond. He smoked angrily and he spoke angrily and his taste in music and art got darker. Every movie he loved was so violent I'd feel sick after watching it. I didn't know how to look anger head-on, and he was covered in it. I knew that everything he felt was justified, but I didn't know where to rest my eyes when I sat across from him.

Eventually, Billy and I stopped meeting for coffee. We stopped talking on the phone.

On the carpet of my bedroom, face close to my boom box speakers, I promised myself that I would always love Ani DiFranco's music. Imagining a life as an adult who wasn't moved by her songs terrified me. *Would I grow up and lose myself?*

Or would I live the kind of life she described—independent and difficult and real, full of fraught romances with men and women, studded with descriptions of surprising beauty. I was in love with her fierceness and her frenetic strums and her voice, which could switch from impossibly soft and sweet to primal in a moment. I listened to the love songs she wrote about other girls and something in me wondered. And then, on the first day of my second semester at college, the wondering was replaced with certainty.

I went to San Francisco State University, where the school's population alone was double that of my hometown, and I relished the anonymity. I remember walking across the campus feeling invisible and free. So when Kristyn strode into the classroom of my women's studies course with a group of friends, joking around, all of them so comfortable with themselves, I didn't have to worry about what anyone would think of me. I didn't have to worry over the way the sight of her sent a jolt to my heart. I was capsized. I was sure. It took me another year—and the miracle of one more class together—to work up the courage to talk to her.

My coming out lacked drama. I had a crush on a girl; it was that simple. Amanda and I talked about it on the phone daily—me in San Francisco, her in Tempe, Arizona—and the small group of new friends I made in the city were complicit in the grand scheme of winning her over.

It worked. Kristyn and I started dating, and six years later, in 2008, we were legally married by the state of California.

* * *

By that time, same-sex marriage was legal in the state of California, but we married in the midst of a volatile campaign waged by anti-LGBTQ rights groups and religious organizations that wanted to take the right to marry away from us. While we were planning our wedding and writing our vows and dreaming of our future together, we were also faced with crowds of protestors with signs in support of Prop 8, yet another amendment to our state Constitution that would revoke our rights. We were faced with crowds waving signs every time we drove across town to my parents' house for dinner. Every protestor, a living reminder of homophobia. Every bumper sticker and yard sign, a hate note in my locker.

Once, when exiting the freeway, we saw a Prop 8 sign attached to a fence that was obviously city property. It was bad enough when people had the signs in their own yards, but I couldn't stand the sight of it hanging where it was, as though it belonged there in the city my wife and I had called home for many years, a city that would vote overwhelmingly against it. "Pull over," I told Kristyn, and then I opened the door and ran across the street to tear the sign down. A man in a white truck saw us and pulled over. My heart sped up as he got out.

"Is that sign yours?" he called from across the street.

The campaign's graphics were confusing and offensive: a stick figure family, each of them a different bright color. It was a rainbow family, standing in opposition to gay families. A rainbow family, asking for protection from us, when all we wanted was to be a family together with the same rights and protections as any other family.

"No," I called back. "It's not mine."

"Then why are you taking it down?" he asked.

"Because it's hateful," I yelled, eyes burning. I ripped the sign in half and dashed back to the car. He followed us, aggressively, to my parents' house, slowed as we stopped but then sped away. I was part victorious, part shaken. I was afraid he'd come back and hurt us. I was standing up for myself, but doing so terrified me.

It was a tight race, and we had a lot of allies. As election night grew later, I watched the television graphics of county results coming in, shading the state of California in patches according to how people voted. It was too close to call, and I stayed awake in hope and dread. When it was finally clear that we had lost, despair set in. It was an echo of seeing Billy slammed against his locker, an echo of learning that Billy wasn't coming back to school, an echo of the ways in which people and authorities and institutions fail those of us who need protection, time and time again, until enough of the population finds these failings unacceptable and demands better. But this time the pain and anger were deeper because now it was about me. I couldn't stand silently at the end of a hallway, pretending not to witness it. My wife and I had said our vows and signed our names and celebrated with our families and friends less than a month prior, and we wondered what would happen to our marriage. And even more than that, I felt the poisonous hatred of my fellow Californians. I knew that the vast majority of people in the Bay Area had voted in our favor, but I still found myself consumed by distrust. Every person I worked with, everyone who rang me up at the grocery store or sat around me in cafés, every stranger I interacted with in any small way was now a potential enemy.

No matter how engaged we are, no matter how much we stand up for our neighbors and friends, when we aren't directly affected by injustice we have the luxury of turning away from it. We know that whatever happens, however terrible and however much we care, it won't directly impact our lives. We sympathize, but we don't fully understand until we've feared for our own safety and security, or that of our family members or closest friends. With marriage came security. The knowledge that it would be my legal right to be in my wife's hospital room if she became ill or injured, the knowledge that she could be in mine. With marriage came the certainty that when we had a child, both of our names could be on her birth certificate even though she would only carry the genes of one of us. And now these certainties were shattered.

A few days after Prop 8 passed, I thought of Billy. I hadn't heard from him in years, but there I was, scouring the Internet. His name is a common one, and false leads were everywhere. Finally I found the right Billy on a social networking site designed to reunite classmates. The site was intentionally misleading, making it seem like people were signed up when they weren't, but I wrote him a long message there anyway, despite a lack of a profile picture or any indication that he would receive it. I told him that I had fallen in love with a girl when I was in college and that we had gotten married. By that point I'd had years of practice coming out, but I deleted and retyped the lines over and over. I thought I should say something self-deprecating. It was so convenient that I discovered I was queer when in college in San Francisco instead of our high school. *How nice for you,* I imagined him thinking with his signature smirk.

How are you? I asked him. *I feel bad about how our friendship ended.*

I wanted to hear back from him that he was okay. Happy, even. I wanted him to have a career and a boyfriend. I wanted to know where he lived. I wanted to hear that he'd made it to the other side of those dark days, that he'd grown up and moved on.

I wanted to learn from him. When you have the courage to know who you are, the courage to say it out loud and not hide it, and in return people ridicule and shame and shun you and you are left defeated and afraid—*what happens after?*

I don't know if he ever got my message. I never heard back.

I will be honest with you: My deep fear is that I'm still standing at the other end of a hallway, watching something violent and unjust and struggling to act or make sense of it. I have been on both sides now—that of an observer, understanding injustice but not feeling the impacts of it on my life, and that of the persecuted, knowing that policies and laws will hurt real people, my family among them. But I am far from silent now. I pay attention and I call my senators and I talk about what matters to me in front of large groups of people in schools across the country. That grief I felt when Billy left our school and again when Prop 8 was passed—the profound cruelty and wrongness of them— returned on November 8, 2016, as the night grew later and the results were clear. And I've felt that way ever since.

Something about the feeling makes me want to connect to that girl on her bedroom carpet or walking the corridors of her high school, headphones on, aware of the way she doesn't belong. I remember the delicateness of my realizations: that some boys who act nice are also cruel, that the school administration didn't care enough to hold on to Billy.

In a way I was fortunate that my understanding of the world was formed by these early disillusionments. Thanks to those experiences, it was horrifying and gut-wrenching but not entirely unexpected that almost half the voting population—not only blatant bigots but also seemingly *nice* people, those who, I imagine, bring dinner to neighbors during times of need and read their children bedtime stories and even profess to care about the innate worth of all people—rallied behind a terrible man. In doing so, they denied the humanity of so many of us.

The other night I listened to "Untouchable Face" for the first time in a long time.

Near the end of the song, Ani DiFranco describes the shifting arrangements of balls on a pool table as a changing constellation. She sees the shape of Orion, but says nothing to the person she's with. With the next shot of the pool cue the constellation will be gone.

I think about Billy and me this way.

A smart, funny boy with a secret.

Gone.

A girl burning with ideas but too afraid to raise her hand in class.

Gone.

The moment he came out to me, all sweaty palms and blushing cheeks.

Gone.

That glimpse of Billy in the hallway, the books on the floor, the tears on his face.

Gone.

Our café meet-ups, the conversations that faded to silences.

Gone.

The particular people we were when we knew each other.

Gone.

These were moments in our lives, and then the moments were over and we went on living. Just as we keep on living now, in this frightening and confusing era, through the persecution of so many people, because when you take religious minorities and people of color and immigrants and LGBTQIA+ people and refugees and survivors of sexual assault and those living with disabilities or illnesses both seen and unseen and all of our allies, there are so many more of us, and we are loud and powerful and galvanized against the fear and prejudice of our countrymen.

A few days ago I looked Billy up again. I scrolled through pictures of strangers with his name, all of them unfamiliar. They were doctors and prisoners, teachers and fishermen. They were much too old or much too young or the right age but with the wrong face.

I wonder if he still goes to shows, if he still smells like clove cigarettes, what color his hair is, if he continued to study French. He learned years before I did how cruel people can be. How they can turn against you because of who you are. But he also learned years before I did how powerful it is to be yourself, to share that with the world.

To say, *Like me or not, here I am, and I am worthy.*

Billy, thank you for showing me how to fight. Wherever you are, I send you my love.

THE ONE WHO DEFINES ME

Aisha Saeed

I was ten years old the first time it happened.

Lacy, Dustin, and Kelly cornered me during recess, frowns etched across their foreheads, hands on their hips.

"We just wanted to know," Lacy asked. "Why did your uncle start a war?"

I blinked. My uncle worked at a computer firm in Maryland.

"You know," Lacy prompted. "The guy in Iraq. Saddam Hussein."

I can't remember much else about that day. I couldn't tell you if the sun was shining or if it was cloudy. I can't even remember what I mumbled in response. But I remember the way they stared at me, expecting an explanation and an apology. I was born in Miami, Florida. My parents immigrated from Pakistan years before I was born and I had no idea who Saddam Hussein was, but that day it didn't seem to matter to them. I remember their glares. I remember the shame I felt.

That was my first time. It was not my last time.

"Does your family own a camel?"

"Do you bathe in sand?"

"Will your dad kill you if you don't listen to him?"

Questions like this followed me through middle school and well into high school, and they weren't just from students.

I was fifteen years old when the Oklahoma City bombing happened. The one where a terrorist blew up a federal building with a bomb. We watched the news in American History. My teacher paced red-faced in the front of the classroom until his eyes landed on me. He paused. He marched up to me.

"When we find out which country did this," he told me, "we will bomb them until there isn't a flower left blooming."

A few days later the terrorist was revealed to be a white American man named Timothy McVeigh. Class resumed without fanfare.

My parents grew up in Pakistan, where nearly everyone else was Muslim just like them. They personally had no experience growing up facing discrimination for one's faith, and because I did not want to put more burdens on their busy shoulders, I never told them what I went through. I also never confided in my friends, nervous they might hear the hateful words and suddenly see me in a new way.

When I graduated high school things improved. I was accepted to the University of Florida, a diverse school with forty thousand students. In this huge melting pot, I was no longer the only Muslim girl in school. There were many different people from all walks of life, including many American Muslims who uniquely understood the things I had gone through. While hateful comments were still made when I wrote op-eds for our college newspaper on matters of race and faith, with a strong support network, it was easier to deflect them.

Then came September 11, 2001.

I had just graduated. It was my third week as a teacher. Reeling from the images pouring out on the office television, I walked toward the lunchroom to get my students, wondering how I would manage to teach anything that day. A substitute teacher stopped me on my way. He gripped my hand in his and told me, "I want you to know, I am not angry with you." I was confused. He had substituted for me the week before, when I'd had a doctor's appointment. Just how badly did my students behave? I almost apologized but paused when his eyes welled up. "I spoke with my wife on the phone, and both she and I don't blame you at all for 9/11." I remember his hands on mine and the numbness that took over me. Someone felt the need to tell me they didn't blame me for the most heinous attack to take place on American soil in recent history. I realized that day not all hurtful comments intend to hurt.

In the months that followed I understood where that

substitute teacher's misguided well intentions came from. It began to feel like the whole country was my high school classroom, a teacher pointing their finger at me in accusation. A boy I'd met just a short while before 9/11 understood exactly how I felt. As a Pakistani American growing up in rural South Carolina, he had many of his own stories to share. There is power in sharing one's painful experiences and voicing them out loud. Even though the stain will always remain, talking helps you air out the hurt. It helps you feel understood and gives you the strength to keep on. I married that boy the following summer.

In the scheme of things, I didn't have it as bad as others I knew. My husband's best friend, who was attending college in the United States on a sports scholarship, went to Pakistan to visit his parents for winter break. When he arrived at the airport, officials told him his visa was revoked and he could never come back. He was one semester away from graduating. I know people who were deported. I have friends, American citizens, who are lawyers and doctors, who have been body-slammed and kicked off flights for appearing suspicious (code word for they had a beard or wore a head scarf). I know people, American citizens, detained and questioned for hours. I have had to stand next to my younger brother, a doctor, and watch as airport personnel enacted three layers of security because his very common name has been placed on a no-fly list.

All my life, as a child, as a teenager, and then as an adult, discrimination was a part of how things were. It was like that annoying little pebble that might get into your shoe at the beach, the one you can't shake off, the one that scrapes and pinches at your heel, but you learn to live with it. That's what living with constant bigotry feels like for me.

But it wasn't all gloom and doom. After 9/11, President George W. Bush visited a mosque. He went out of his way to make a formal statement that the attack that happened was committed by people who warped their notions of Islam and that their actions did not in any way speak for the peaceful Muslims and Muslim countries he knew and respected. He assured Muslim Americans they were welcome and valued in this country. While many things happened during his administration that I disagree with profoundly, and Muslims did in fact experience a lot of difficulties and unspeakable situations during those years, I do now realize the value of the leader of my country taking a public stand for members of my faith.

The day after Barack Obama was elected president, I cried tears of joy at my law office with my colleagues. We couldn't believe it. We'd made history and elected the first Black US president. During his term he stopped NSEERS (a database created under George W. Bush that profiled and targeted Muslims) and tried to close down Guantanamo Bay. And while there were certainly many things to improve upon and work on, it felt like slowly we were moving past discrimination as a country; we were going to be greater than hate.

Fast-forward to November 8, 2016, the day the United States of America elected a man endorsed by the KKK, whose primary campaign promise was to ban Muslims from the country. I cried once again following the election, but this time my tears were anything but joyful. I watched as he laid out an executive order to ban Muslims. As a US citizen, this ban would not affect me, but the message he was sending was clear: We don't like Muslims. We don't want Muslims. My existence was something they had to grin and bear, for now.

The election shook my understanding of my community. I knew there were misconceptions and prejudice, yes, but to elect a man so openly and vehemently against my existence? I wondered: Who were my neighbors? My colleagues? My community? I paused at the produce aisle at the grocery store. Did the man who restocked the cabbages and smiled at my children also vote for a man who wished to erase my family?

The weekend following the election, I went to a book festival in Charleston, South Carolina, with my family. On Friday, en route to the festival, we stopped at a halfway point, a fast-food restaurant in a small town, to get a bite to eat. All the customers—I wish I was kidding—every single one, turned to us and glared. A teenager began taking pictures of us and sharing with her friends. I wondered if I was imagining things until my husband abruptly suggested we take our food to go. Stepping into the parking lot, we saw the cars and understood. Each one had a bumper sticker supporting the new president. Several had

Confederate flags flying from their windows. Their glares made the message clear: we didn't belong there.

That Saturday a group of men in line at a club chanted "Make American Great Again" as I walked past them. I saw a truck making rounds every hour with a Confederate flag the size of a table flying from its truck bed as the driver screamed out *"America!"* as though it belonged only to him. In line to get dinner later that evening at an authors-only event at the festival, a fellow author insulted me and my husband and then told us she could speak to us any way she wanted now that Donald Trump was president.

I grew up with bigotry. I was used to being painted the Other, but until now it was something that was usually subtle, that happened quietly behind closed doors, computer screens, or when people thought no one was listening. I had not received this kind of open vitriol since I was a child. Now it seemed bigots were given a blank check to unleash their hatred as they saw fit as openly as they wished.

The Sunday following the election I spent time with my family and walked through the historic city of Charleston. My mother-in-law, who lived nearby, joined us. She's a proud Muslim woman who also happens to wear hijab, a headscarf. I noticed the silent stares along the walkways. I saw cars slow down, the passengers turning to watch her walk past. I saw people stealing glances at her in the stores. Not all the looks were malicious. Most were curious. In that moment I realized some of these people may never have seen a visibly Muslim woman before. It is easier to consider us inhuman when you have not ever seen us beyond the scary headlines and the rhetoric of the leader of the country. If all they knew were scary images of oppressed women with overbearing men watching over, what did they make of my mother-in-law in a pink headscarf tickling my children and deciding which bath soaps she wanted to buy from the little boutique in the corner of the city? I asked my mother-in-law if she felt uncomfortable by the constant looks. If she wondered if they were looking at her curiously or with hate in their hearts. She looked up at me puzzled by the question. "No," she told me. "That's their business. Not mine."

Life has a way of presenting you with the same lessons over and over again until you finally get it. That weekend was an important weekend for me because I finally learned something that the universe had been trying to teach me for a long time and showed me in my mother-in-law. The lesson was simple: though the rhetoric against my humanity has ramped up, the rhetoric has always been there and it does not and should not define my humanity. No matter how loudly someone says I don't matter and no matter how much conviction they put into those words, or try to blame me for things that are not in my control, their feelings are not based in reality; they are based in bigotry and they are wrong.

I wish I'd known this lesson as a teen. That I am not defined by what others think of me. I define myself. I am a unique individual among a group of 1.7 billion Muslims around the globe. While I admire many Muslims, such as the late and great Muhammad Ali, basketball all-star Shaquille O'Neal, and the pop singer Zayn Malik (oh yes, he's Muslim too) they are not me and I am not them. They cannot speak for me, nor can I speak for them. And that is the same of any other person who says they are Muslim and do anything, whether it is good or bad.

I am Aisha. I like doodling and chocolate. I like baking and pedicures. I get grumpy when I'm hungry, and I like hiking even though I'm slow at it and everyone always leaves me behind. I adore my KitchenAid mixer more than anyone ever should, and I find peace when I press my head to the ground and pray. I am a fully actualized human being no matter what people say about me.

This doesn't mean the things people say don't hurt. They do. I would be lying if I said reading an article lambasting the entire Muslim faith, and by consequence me, doesn't twist at my heart. I've learned to accept that feeling too. It shows me that my heart still beats. It shows me I still care about things, and it drives me to make things better. Having a tender spot is not anything to be ashamed of, but now I also don't let it soak into me. I feel the sting and I move on. I will not allow those who hate to live rent-free in my head, and I take that hate and I rechannel it into working to create good in the world.

As difficult as things are, I take time to enjoy my life and appreciate my blessings and also take my responsibility as a citizen more seriously than I ever have before. I call my representatives. I write them. I reach out to my friends who are hurting and scared and hold their hands. I write books featuring Muslim characters, who resemble less the stereotypes the media and television has put out for years and more the people I grew up loving and knowing. There is only one way to change the world, and that is by each of us doing what we can, using our strengths and our gifts to help make the world the world we want to see.

Muslims are part of the fabric of our country. I am part of the fabric of this country. I owe no one any apologies or explanations for who I am. While things will get difficult in the years to come, it is this I know to hold tight to: we define ourselves, we do not let the bigotry of others define us, and we work hard to create the world we want.

If we keep doing this, we will get through this. You. And me.

IN OUR GENES

Hannah Moskowitz

My mother is really big on genealogy. She has her family traced back to Charlemagne. Her side has French princesses, William Penn, and some-number-of-great-grandparents who arrived on the *Mayflower*. Every time she finds the name of a new relative, she can trace someone new, and someone new again. It never stops.

My mother was born in rural North Carolina in 1957, raised by a young mother who gave her the initials KKK and such sage advice growing up as, "Never put money in your mouth; a Black person might have touched it" (and you better believe she did not say "Black person"). I joke that that's why she got engaged when she was seventeen—not to my father, but to a nice Southern boy—to try to change her last name as soon as possible.

But she didn't marry that nice Southern boy. She married a second-generation Jewish guy named Saul, who was in North Carolina for law school, and became the first person in her family, going back thousands and thousands of years, to marry a non-Christian.

She has, of course, tried to do my dad's genealogy. It's a lot more difficult and a lot more depressing. Contrasting my mom, who's had family in America since the moment white people starting stomping around, my dad's grandparents were immigrants. His grandmother came from Hungary to get away from her abusive father. His grandfather came from Russia to get away from the pogroms. Everyone they left behind either lived through the Holocaust, or didn't.

My mom traded her KKK initials for a clunky Jewish last name and learned the Hanukkah blessing—or most of it; she still gets tongue-tied at the end—but she never converted. They had two kids—my older sister, and me.

Traditionally, Judaism is matrilineal. People like to tell me this like it's going to be new information. (Reform Judaism has accepted children with Jewish fathers since 1983—eight years before I was born—but people who are sticklers for rules and tradition don't tend to respect my branch of Judaism anyway.) Of the four members of my family, I'm the only practicing Jew. My mother says that instead of having two half-Jewish kids, they had one Jewish kid and one non-Jewish kid.

It was actually kind of a shock to me the first time she said this, because the fact that I actually practiced Judaism wasn't something I'd ever shared with her. My first semester of college I fell in with a bunch of Jewish friends who had all been raised distinctively Jewish but loved me despite my non-bat-mitzvahed ass, and I went to Hillel with them. I felt self-conscious that I was the only one who needed the Hebrew transliteration, but I kept going. I hadn't told my mother any of this—she wears her disdain for religion with the pride only a Southern atheist can—but she let out this little quip about having one Jewish child and one non-Jewish when we were a couple margaritas deep with a few panelists I'd just been on a women-in-publishing panel with. She'd come up to New York with me because I was nineteen and she was my best friend.

It was an incredible moment, and it was heartwarming and it was confirming, this shock of being seen. When I tell her nowadays about going to temple, she still doesn't understand why I do it, but it doesn't surprise her. She's known me, after all, for longer than I've known me.

Which was part of what made it so surprising when I came over to her house to see her, at twenty years old, and told her I was in a relationship with a girl, and she looked at me like her world had dropped out from under her. I'd been with girls for a year; she really didn't know?

Or was it that it really took her nineteen years to come to terms with having a Jewish child, and I hadn't yet given her that for having a queer one?

Seriously, nineteen fucking years?

I've been thinking about my mother a lot lately. About the people she came from, who either didn't notice (her theory) or intentionally chose (you gotta wonder . . .) to give her the initials they gave her. About where she grew up and what she was told. And how, despite all that, she married my father. She knit pink hats for the Women's March in 2017. She has stood beside me and cheered "Black lives matter" like she was someone who was not raised to believe that they did not.

I think about the discomfort on her face when I want to talk about anti-Semitism. It's very hard for her to accept that that is still happening in the world, because she was raised on a diet of steady, subtle racism, not hate crimes. I can't ever tell her about getting harassed online, because her immediate question is, *What did you do?* because she has never been a target simply for existing. She's not present online the way I am. She doesn't know people outside of our liberal community and her mother, whom she very rarely speaks to.

A few years ago, when her father was dying, she had to go down to North Carolina a lot. Her parents had a nasty divorce— he was a Connecticut liberal; I honestly don't know how they lasted five minutes around each other, never mind a twenty-five-year marriage—but, ever the devoted daughter, my mother still stayed at my grandmother's house when she went down to see her dad. More often than not, the trips would involve them screaming at each other about politics, and my mother would come home insecure, asking me if I *really* liked her haircut, because her mother had spent all week criticizing it. I fall apart when my mother criticizes me too, but that's just about the only similarity in our relationships.

My mother has come so far.

But then she asks me what I did to deserve getting harassed online, and she rolls her eyes if someone mentions the Holocaust, and she stands there gaping when I tell her I'm dating a girl . . .

I get so mad.

She was a stay-at-home mom. She did PTA. She packed my lunch every day all through high school. I love my dad with everything in me, but between her and my sister and the incredible women I have dated, I am a woman who has been grown by women.

(This, by the way, is why I will never understand women who say they "don't need feminism" while they sit on the shoulders of women who did, but okay.)

My mom has come so far. Look at that shitty town in North Carolina. Look at what they named her. Look at the generations and generations and generations of people who never would have looked twice at my father, or worse.

She did not think, when she married my father, that she would have kids who'd get death threats for having his last name, but I do. I have a block list on Twitter thirteen thousand names long, and I still get a few threats a week for my sin of being online with my name. My mother's on Twitter now too, with our last name, and I worry about her. Nothing's happened to her yet.

And she will fight for gay rights all day long, but she never thought it would be for the baby she carried and brought home from the hospital and made lunches for every day. I know. It's hard for me to understand my queerness as a shock, but I try to think about if I have children, what ways they'll have to shock me. What they'll discover about themselves that right now I don't even know is an option.

I want my mother to be perfect. But more than that, I want her to be enough. I want all of the work that she's done, all of the incredible growing up she has had to do alone—my mother is a woman who was grown into the amazing person she is by and large by one woman and that woman is *herself*—to be enough, because maybe she can't do any more. She has come so, so far.

She just has this daughter she wasn't prepared for.

And isn't that kind of what's happening to a lot of us right now?

My mother was not prepared for me. And it was a lot easier to judge her for that before this year. Because I was not prepared. And unless someone has every possible intersection of every possible marginalized person, there is something going on right now that they were not prepared for either.

At the Women's March, beside my mother, I looked around at signs about refugees and the Dakota Access Pipeline. I talk to teenagers on Twitter who are struggling to have their genders and sexualities validated and protected. These are the people that I was not expecting in my life. These are the mothers and sisters and daughters that I was not trained for. I might be more marginalized than my mother, but I'm more privileged than a *lot* of others. And I might not be related to the people I trip over when I fail to use the right words or see things from the right perspective, but that doesn't make my mistakes less hurtful.

What if I can't be good enough either?

But I have to be. I have to be better.

Look at how far my mother came. Look at the head start I have.

I am on the shoulders of every single woman who came before me. I am on the strong, sign-wielding back of a woman who did so much heavy lifting, who overcame so much shit, to start me off in a place where I can nitpick her advocacy.

Which I will do, at the same time I appreciate her, because this is my job. This is what daughters have to do. We have to go even further. Be even better. And teach the next ones to be better than us. This is the definition of progress.

Hundreds of years in the future, when some girl is doing her genealogy, make her goddamn proud.

AN ACCIDENTAL ACTIVIST

Ellen Hopkins

If you follow me on social media, you know I'm a political beast. I make no bones about how I lean, which is hard to the left. I'm a staunch believer in the equal rights our Constitution affords every American, regardless of religion, skin color, country of origin, gender, or sexual identity. And if our president and congresspersons don't represent every one of us equally, I am willing to openly and vocally call them out, or take to the streets and march, if required. Activism is second nature to me. That might not surprise you. But how I became engaged with it just might.

Honestly, I define "white privilege." I was adopted as a baby by an older couple. My dad was seventy-two and my mom was forty-two when they brought me home from the hospital where I was ushered into this world. Daddy, the son of German immigrants, was born in San Francisco in 1883. His family was poor and so was his education, which only went through the sixth grade. But he was a brilliant man and willing to work hard, something he did every day of his life until he passed away at eighty-seven years old. Over his lifetime he set a world record in the long jump, invented a bookkeeping system, and built several businesses. One of those was a steel-manufacturing company that provided necessary resources to the government during World War II, and with it came a fair amount of money. My father defined "self-made man" and the American dream.

We weren't Rockefeller rich, but we lived comfortably in an affluent Palm Springs, California, neighborhood. To escape the sweltering summer heat, we traveled north to Napa and Lake Tahoe. My childhood passions, which my parents supported, were horses, dance, and books, in that order. We attended church every Sunday. Our regular congregations were Presbyterian and Lutheran, but sometimes we'd attend Catholic or Baptist services, and my best friend in grade school was Jewish, so once in a while I'd tag along to her synagogue. There was never a concept of "one true religion" in our home.

I went to an exceptional non-parochial private school, with excellent teachers who encouraged critical thinking skills. Looking back, I see that three of my favorites happened to be gay men, but I had no clue about that then. It wasn't something people talked about in the sixties, certainly not around children. Nor was it a badge worn out and proudly. Gay people stayed in their closets, except in certain urban areas where they felt safe among their brothers and sisters.

Neither was I very aware of the Civil Rights Movement occurring around the country. While I'd learned a little about the Civil War and slavery, I'd had no idea about the escalating African-American fight for social justice in the intervening years. As a child of white privilege, the violence and fear Black kids faced every day in their own neighborhoods was a foreign concept to me. It had never touched me. I'd never seen it. It was as if we lived on different planets.

The only political event I knew about in grade school was John F. Kennedy's assassination. America's thirty-fifth president served less than three years before Lee Harvey Oswald shot him on November 22, 1963. The United States was at odds (verging on war) with the Soviet Union and Cuba, so some people believed one or the other was behind a bigger plot. Others thought the Mafia, the CIA, or even Vice President Lyndon B. Johnson might have played a role, though investigators concluded Oswald acted alone. Regardless, the trajectory of this country changed with JFK's death. Many historians agree he likely would've sought a diplomatic solution to the Vietnam conflict, while his successor escalated the war.

I was eight years old on that November day, so while I understood the basic details, the speculation about motives was completely lost on me. My parents might have discussed it, and I'm sure the nightly news played in the background, but the importance of that moment in time was something I came to understand later.

My parents were Republicans. My dad was a businessman, after all. But they weren't overtly political. Rarely did I hear them talk about elections or candidates or how they felt about the draft that was sending boys to Vietnam in the sixties. My first real taste of politics came in the eighth grade, when we did mock elections. We drew names of candidates to research, and my pick was Robert F. Kennedy, John's younger brother. The year was 1968.

I learned that Bobby Kennedy served as JFK's attorney general, and in that role he advocated for the civil rights of African-Americans. In 1962, he sent federal troops to Oxford, Mississippi, to enforce a US Supreme Court order admitting the first Black student, James Meredith, to the University of Mississippi. The state's segregationist governor, Ross Barnett, had tried to bar Meredith, whose enrollment provoked demonstrations at the school. Bobby also worked, first with his brother and then with President Lyndon Johnson, on the landmark Civil Rights Act of 1964, which outlawed racial discrimination in voting, employment, and public facilities.

This was my introduction to the Civil Rights Movement in the United States, as well as to major players, including Martin Luther King Jr. and Malcolm X. It was my first clear realization of the struggle for racial parity in a country that was supposed to guarantee equal rights for all.

On the day MLK was assassinated, Bobby Kennedy was scheduled to give a campaign speech in inner-city Indianapolis. Despite fear of violence, he broke the news of Dr. King's death and comforted the largely Black audience with what has been called one of the great public addresses of the modern era. He acknowledged and honored their anger, but reminded them of King's own efforts to "replace that violence, that stain of bloodshed that has spread across our land, with an effort to understand with compassion and love."

His words resonated with a girl on the brink of adolescence, as did the marches and protests and even the riots that inevitably followed. At thirteen, I became a Democrat because Bobby Kennedy spoke about things my heart insisted were true. And when he was gunned down in June of that year, his death affected me deeply. He died for what he believed in. That powerful message resonated, but I never confessed this to my parents.

My dad, for all his many fine traits, was undeniably the "king of his castle." His generation held more respect for men than for women, who weren't welcomed into the workforce, except in certain specific roles: teachers, nurses, secretaries. My mother, in fact, met my father when she applied for a receptionist job at his factory. He was a widower, having lost his wife of forty years to lung cancer. Mama, who had worked as a nurse/caretaker for two decades, was in need of a job after her longtime patient passed away. Daddy was lonely. Mama was hungry. He was powerful. She was deferential. I can't speak to romance, but somehow they agreed to marry.

It was a rocky relationship. My father was what I call a weekend alcoholic. Didn't touch a drop from Sunday morning until Friday evening, when he'd start drinking and stay mostly drunk through Saturday night. Regardless, he'd be up on time for church. Weekdays were relatively quiet, but alcohol-fueled arguments were common on Daddy's days off, and those were the only times I ever heard my mom voice opinions that ran counter to her husband's. Women were supposed to be seen and not listened to.

But I loved listening to her. Our shared pastime was horse-back riding, and on long desert jaunts, she'd tell me about her history or confide aspirations. Had she lived in another time, she would have accomplished great things, I believe. I remember an invention of hers, dreamed up to save time in the kitchen. But she didn't have the resources to actually patent and build trash compactors, which appeared several years later. My mom was bright, funny, and compassionate. That I was one of the few people who were allowed to see those things in her confounded me. And to witness her societally programmed obedience to my father's will likely sparked my early resistance to the concept of male dominion.

Mama also loved literature, especially the classics, though she was not above enjoying a bit of pulp fiction from time to time. She inspired my love of reading, and never censored a thing. In fact, she encouraged me to read widely, knowing books would open my eyes to a world much larger than the relatively protected one in which we lived. I pored through chapter books before kindergarten. By sixth grade, I devoured everything from *Lord of the Rings* to *Lord of the Flies*.

Once I hit high school, it was anything I could get my hands on, and in digesting classics like D. H. Lawrence's *Lady Chatterley's Lover* and Nathaniel Hawthorne's *The Scarlet Letter*, it dawned on me how women have been pigeonholed throughout history. More modern, and even sexier fare, including Erica Jong's *Fear of Flying* and Pauline Réage's *Story of O*, showed me that women could choose not only to embrace their gender, but also use it to accomplish their goals. This made me confront the uncomfortable concept of patriarchy within religion, something I struggled to reconcile with the idea of an all-accepting God. As I came to terms with this, and also embraced my awakening sexuality, I decided that the time had come to break free of tradition. Feminism was taking root, not only in society but also in me.

High school, in fact, is where I first fell into activism. We had moved to the Santa Ynez Valley the summer after I graduated from the eighth grade. It was, and remains, quintessential small-town California—rolling hills and oak trees, ranch land (much of which is now planted in vineyards), and perfectly pretty neighborhoods. Almost all the kids in the high school had known one another since childhood, which put newcomer me on the fringes of the student body. I didn't mind so much. Despite being a straight-A student, "mainstream" didn't appeal to me.

Truthfully, I was born a rebel, and my teen years illustrate that. Sometimes I ditched classes, and I got really good at forging absence slips. (Luckily, I didn't need lectures to ace tests.) I was comfortable with my body and didn't mind displaying it at nude beaches and swimming holes. ("Look, but don't touch" was the rule, and my German shepherd enforced it.) I preferred hanging out with guys to having sex with them (with a couple of notable exceptions). Okay, I smoked weed (but it was rare for me to drink alcohol).

I chose to avoid alcohol because, at home and outside of it, I saw how drinking to excess could make men aggressive and women compliant. I was determined to remain on equal footing with the guys in my life and was fortunate to find male companions who accepted my parameters. One of them, whom I loved very much, was killed in a drunk driving accident. At sixteen, I suffered real loss for the first time. My dad passed away not long after, and my mom's subsequent tailspin proved how dependent on him she was. I vowed never to be totally reliant on a partner, and I'm proud to have managed that over the years. I've made mistakes, but nothing I couldn't recover from.

Rebel or no, I did manage to make some amazing friends and go out with some very cute guys. A couple of those friends lost brothers in the Vietnam War, which was in its waning years at the time. Still, several boys who were close to me were sweating the draft. I'll never forget them waiting for the Selective Service lottery that put them in danger of being forced into the armed services and shipped overseas. The evening news showed footage of men conscripted to kill or be killed in the jungles of Indochina. We saw graphic photos of bombed villages, fallen soldiers, and massacred villagers.

In the years since, the role of television coverage in the public debate about the Vietnam War has been dissected again and again. It was the first American conflict where some 90 percent of the country's households owned TVs, and as primitive as the technology was, still we were escorted, via the screen, to a war-ravaged part of the world few enough of us would otherwise see. Some claim media spin was responsible for the surge in anti-war sentiment. Others insist that without the undeniable evidence of events like the Mai Lai Massacre (where American soldiers eliminated a village of South Vietnamese civilians) such atrocities would have continued. What can't be denied is that visual connection brought the human element of combat into clear focus.

There were anti-war rallies across the country, people rising up in protest of what they felt was an unjust conflict. I admired the shared vision and their willingness to go to jail if that's what it took to be heard. On April 30, 1970, President Richard Nixon announced the US invasion of Cambodia. This led to massive demonstrations, including one on the campus of Kent State University in Ohio. On May 4, students armed only with sticks and rocks clashed with Ohio State National Guardsmen, who opened fire, killing four young protestors and wounding nine. When I heard this news it was like being punched in the gut, though

I didn't know any of the victims personally. And it was there this accidental activist was born. I was fifteen.

In our small, conservative valley, there were no marches. No overt demonstrations. But some friends and I figured out a way to make our voices heard—through silence. We refused to stand for the daily Pledge of Allegiance we were expected to participate in every morning. My homeroom overseer, who happened to be an ex-military shop teacher, was not amused and sent us to the principal's office. Mr. Silva lectured us on the importance of respect for our country and its flag.

I reminded him of those dead Kent State students and asked how, exactly, their corpses represented "liberty and justice for all." He suggested protestors weren't true Americans and reiterated his expectation that I would stand for the Pledge the next morning. I asked him if he was aware of this thing called the First Amendment, something I believed applied to everyone, even outspoken young people like myself. He told me he did not appreciate my attitude and warned that if I chose not to comply my name would be added to a "watch list." Anti-war activism was considered unpatriotic.

"Patriotism," I insisted, "means holding your country to the highest standard. Killing innocent civilians, either here in the States or over there in the jungle, is pretty damn low." Maybe I touched a nerve. He didn't suspend me. But when I continued to sit for the Pledge, my name was added to his watch list. I have to admit taking pride in that.

In addition to countless individual protests like mine, there were huge demonstrations, including one in 1967 where one hundred thousand people gathered at the Lincoln Memorial in Washington D.C. Joining college students were members of the Vietnam Veterans Against the War. Many were in wheelchairs, and watching them on television, throwing away the medals they'd earned, encouraged "regular folk" into the anti-war effort. Perhaps for the first time in this country's history a majority of the American people stood together against the government's foreign policy. In 1973, caving to a strong anti-war mandate, President Richard Nixon announced the effective end to US involvement in Southeast Asia. And I played a small but memorable role.

As the war wound down, a new movement caught my interest. The proposed Equal Rights Amendment (ERA) would guarantee freedom from legal discrimination due to gender. The idea that women weren't protected from bias in the workplace and elsewhere made no sense to me, but even today women aren't assured the same pay as men doing the same job. One reason is because, even though the proposed Twenty-Seventh Amendment to the Constitution passed both the House of Representatives and the Senate in 1972, it was not ratified by the required thirty-eight states. To this day, there is still nothing in the Constitution ensuring equal rights for women.

But as women lobbied for ratification, I was swept along. Immersing myself in the history of American women's struggles was eye-opening. From the first Women's Rights Convention in 1848 through the suffrage movement that resulted in women finally earning the right to vote in 1920 (only white women, however; it took the Civil Rights Movement to enfranchise Black women and men), up to and including the ERA, the fight for gender egalitarianism has been an uphill battle. The more I learned, the more frustrated I became, and it sparked the torch of feminism I've carried throughout my life.

As an interesting aside, the state of Nevada, which I've called home for thirty years, just voted to ratify the Twenty-Seventh Amendment. Though beyond the original time frame allowed for ratification, there may be some legal precedence to pass the ERA, even now, should enough states join the Silver State in supporting gender equality. So maybe the signs I carried forty-odd years ago will still matter.

Over those decades, I've become a staunch advocate for many causes, chief among them LGBTQ rights. Yes, my oldest child happens to be gay, but the bigger reason is, from the time Bobby Kennedy spoke to my conscience until now, I have believed that equal rights for every single person in this country is not only promised by our Constitution, but vital to the health of our society.

I'm a bleeding-heart liberal. I make no apologies for that. And what my heart bleeds for is a viable future for my grandchildren, and their grandchildren, and all the generations to come. The planet is in peril, and activism is more critical now than ever before.

The 2016 election hit me hard because its outcome shattered my core belief in the political process, not to mention the progress this country seemed to have made in the decades immediately preceding it. The potential for human rights violations and environmental degradation is difficult to fathom. That so much of the country supported candidates determined to eliminate programs and agencies designed to protect the very elements required to sustain a decent quality of life on Planet Earth is simply beyond my ken. It hurts to consider how many things we fought for and gained when I was a teen are in jeopardy now.

The good news is America has reawakened. Those of us determined to lobby for the health of our republic and its democratic principles have mobilized and embraced the principle of using our collective voice. In huge numbers, we are calling and e-mailing and tweeting our representatives in government, demanding to be heard. We are overflowing town hall meetings, picking up signs and marching in the streets, reminding this country that democracy must not become a commodity, sold to the highest bidder. Those in power aren't invincible or greater than the will of We the People. We are joining together in protest, and that defines patriotism, because we're fighting for the principles that have always made America great. This gives me hope for the future.

That future is in my hands, and yours. I call on you to hoist the banner of activism. Find a cause (or two) that matters to you, whether it's animal rights or LGBTQ rights, public lands or public schools, clean energy or clean water. Develop a real understanding of the stakes. Learn who your legislators are and how to open dialogues with them. State your concerns clearly and succinctly, and never forget that your representatives are supposed to work for you, regardless of political party affiliation.

Most of all, as soon as you're eligible, register to vote, and cherish that right. Vote! In every single election, including midterms and primaries, not to mention state and local contests, which can be decided by a handful of votes. Be sure you are registered and have in place any state-required ID. Take the time to research candidates and ballot measures. These will affect you, negatively or positively. The choice is yours, and the ballot is key. Never, ever believe your voice doesn't matter. It is powerful and necessary to the survival of your values. And while you're at it, encourage others to get out to the polls. Elections have been won or lost by very small margins, 2016 included. Had a few more people decided not to stay home, the outcome might have been very different.

I stumbled into activism almost fifty years ago, and never left. Please join me. No matter how you arrive, accidentally or purposefully, hold fast to your ideals. Visualize the tomorrow you want to be part of. And never stop fighting for it.

DREAMS DEFERRED AND OTHER EXPLOSIONS

Ilene (I.W.) Gregorio

I don't remember exactly when I started hating my name, but I suspect it happened, like so many childhood traumas, on the school bus. It may have been the first time a kid called me "Ching-Chong Wong." Or the time a girl I had never thought of as particularly mean felt compelled to tell me the old joke: "How does a Chinese person name their kid? By throwing forks down a stairway." More likely, it was any of the thousand times someone made a pun about me going the "Wong way."

Even as a child, I understood that my name was not my identity, but it sure as heck was a prism through which people saw me.

As a teenager, I called bullshit on Shakespeare's famous

quote: "A rose by any other name would smell as sweet." My name was not some meaningless signifier. It wasn't a mere collection of letters. It was a brand, labeling me as an "other" in my otherwise Wonder Bread–white Central New York town.

I learned, over the years, that my name brings with it certain expectations.

First, there are the obvious physical expectations: the color of my hair, the shape of my eyes, my body type. Then there are the expectations of what subjects I excel at in school, which ones I'm hopeless at, and whether I play an instrument. It brings with it assumptions about my work ethic, how I will interact with people, even my financial savvy.

This isn't to say that there weren't ways the specific expectations of being Asian benefited me. I will never have an airline employee ask for my medical license when I raise my hand to answer a call for a doctor on a flight. I'll never be denied a loan because of the color of my skin. I don't think I've ever walked down a sidewalk and had a stranger cross the street to avoid me.

Sometimes I don't know if it's better when I meet these expectations, or worse, because it makes me wonder how much choice I had in the paths I chose, in the person I've become. Have I grown into the shape of my name, the way a tree's roots spread and become molded into the shape of the pot in which it sits?

I graduated from college a walking cliché: an Ivy League–

educated, former-violin-playing Asian-American student heading to medical school. One could say that I fulfilled the destiny of my name; my graduation cards should have said "Congratulations! You have met expectations!"

This is not to say that I fit perfectly into the stereotype. In some ways I am incredibly lazy. I rarely practiced that previously mentioned violin of my own volition. I am at times careless with my money. I'm a horrible daughter who never has time to call her family. I love eating to the point where I have a bit of a muffin top, but I can barely cook. I suck at statistics, and my husband handles all the IT in our household.

The writer in me would say that idiosyncrasies like these are what make me rounded, fully fleshed out, and human. My analytical side accepts this without question, even as my inner child hesitates. Because when the expectation is to fit perfectly into a mold, little defects can make you feel, well, defective.

Food, for instance: I love it in a primal, uncontrollable way that is best exhibited at dim sum restaurants, where I've been known to lunge out of my seat to flag down a tray of pineapple custard buns. Yet my entire life, this source of joy has been tainted with guilt.

Each year, when my mother comes to visit from Taiwan, one of the first things my husband and I do is take bets on how many minutes it will take for my mom to make a comment about how our weight has changed since the last time she saw us. Over the years, I've gotten used to her signature move—reaching out to grab and fondle the flab under my upper arm to get a sense of whether I've been exercising.

The little things my mother would do to manage my body never made sense until the first time I went to China, when I was dismayed to note that I could only fit into "extra-large" clothing. There I was, literally not fitting into the pattern that was meant for me.

My mom's obsession with my weight made further sense in the context of the expectations placed upon the literal bodies of Asian women, like the time I went to get *The Joy Luck Club* at a video store and the checkout clerk said, smirking, "Good movie. Really attractive women." It made sense the first time a friend warned me about a guy who had an eye on me because of his Asian fetish. "He totally has Yellow Fever," she said, explaining that some guys like Asian women because they're "exotic" and submissive. As I've gotten older and learned more about American military history in the Pacific, I've come to understand how these stereotypes came to pass (think *Miss Saigon* and *Memoirs of a Geisha*), and also how insidiously wrong they are. But when I was a teenager, all I could process was, "Oh, they're kind of right." After all, "student is a joy to teach" was the most common comment on my report card, followed closely by "should speak up more in class." I was polite. I was quiet and deferential. I hated it when people were mad at me (still do) and did everything I could to appease and to avoid conflict.

Even—especially—conflicts within myself.

The thing is, I've wanted to be a writer since I was eight years old. Growing up, books were my best friends, my refuge from the loneliness and subtle but omnipresent racism in my conservative town. I have always known that I wanted to be a friend to others through story.

Problem was, Chinese girls weren't writers. With one notable exception (Bette Bao Lord's *In the Year of the Boar and Jackie Robinson*), all of my favorite books growing up were written by white authors. Every. Single. One.

Medicine, on the other hand, was a fully approved career choice, one pursued by my grandfather, my aunt, and two uncles (one on each side) before me. As was my MO, I tried to compromise. Even though I continued writing, I told myself that I could do science writing—that I could follow in the steps of the many physician writers in history (Chekhov! Michael Crichton! Richard Selzer!) to combine my passions. It was a good plan.

The most insidious part of being a model minority is the contortion act, which is sometimes more evident to others than to yourself. When I was applying to medical school, one of my career counselors told me point-blank: "You want to make sure you're not putting a square peg into a round hole." To this day I'm not sure what tipped her off, unless it was my over-rehearsed justification for why I wanted to be a doctor (I wanted to help people, I loved working with people, insert romantic notion of medicine here ____).

Looking back at myself, I can see how badly I was straining for an identity, but how scared I was to invent one that didn't include medicine. I wanted so much to conform to expectations that I brainwashed myself.

This is not to say that going to medical school was, in the end, a bad decision. I enjoy many aspects of medicine. I love most of my patients. Gainful employment and job security are good for mental health. But putting one's dreams into a straitjacket? Not so much.

Langston Hughes asked what happened about dreams deferred, and all of his answers have fit me at one point or another: Drying up like a raisin in the sun. Festering like a sore. Crusting and sugaring over. Sagging like a heavy load. Exploding.

Explosions are by their nature sudden, violent things, but like all expenditures of energy, there's work leading up to the big bang. There's a pressure buildup, a storage of potential energy.

In my life I've had sparks of rebellion against expectation, but they were almost always deeply internal. I read fantasy novels instead of the scientists' biographies my family gave me, buying comic books with my birthday money and hiding them underneath my bed. My father would try to coax me into listening to his old LPs of classical music, but I ignored him and listened to mixtapes of Broadway musicals. Then, in possibly one of my most significant transgressions—at least in the eyes of a family that viewed athletic activity as a complete waste of time—I became a sports fan.

Worse, I chose ice hockey, which is arguably the sport least likely to fit the sensibility of someone who's grown up as the model minority. My introduction to hockey was the scene in *Superfudge* where Peter Hatcher's friend talks about wanting to go to a game so he can see blood bounce on the ice, and of course the stereotype of the sport is that it's a violent, even brutish sport played by large Canadians with anger-management issues.

Which is maybe why a *Highlights* magazine article about a skinny kid named Wayne Gretzky using his brains to lead the league in scoring captured my imagination. While I was attracted at first with the idea that you could be both cerebral *and* athletic, I fell for the game for the same reason Sandy fell for Danny in *Grease*: because it was fast, because it was beautiful, and because it was *dangerous*.

For most of high school, I admired the game from afar. I never went to games, not only because of cost, but because I was too embarrassed to tell my family where I was going. I never even flirted with the idea of playing myself. Ice time is expensive, for one; but the more honest reason was fear of ridicule.

Let's face it: if a short, skinny Asian girl with glasses thicker than the size of her pinkie walked into a hockey rink, you would probably think she was an intern for the local paper. Or maybe shadowing the team doctor. Even if I had had the guts to try out for my high school team, I would never have been any good, what with the sum total of my proven athletic experience being the ability to run short distances at a moderately fast speed.

This idea that a pursuit is valid only if you're able to do it at a level high enough to impress college admission counselors is one of the most insidious pressures on model minority kids. Growing up, the fear of being mediocre prevented me from trying so many things I secretly wanted to do: acting, art, playing the guitar.

There was no way I was going to play hockey under the eye of my family. Then, the summer after I graduated high school, Rollerblades happened. Then ice-skating and low-stakes club sports.

It's not an exaggeration to say that skating was the first time I ever flirted with losing control, the first time I embraced that sense of panic you feel when you're one burst of acceleration away from slipping, when you're a fraction of a millimeter removed from tumbling face-first into unforgiving sideboards.

It turned out that I loved speed, that I got a thrill from the sharp crack of wood hitting wood whenever I fought with abandon for a three-inch piece of rubber and came out victorious with the puck. There is no hitting in women's hockey, but there's still a striking physicality, a struggle for possession, and a general lack of inhibition. There's a fearlessness you have to have in playing hockey that allowed me to acknowledge—even welcome—my nasty side.

If the perks of being a model minority include a general security against racial profiling, the downsides include a visceral aversion to rocking the boat. I went through most of my education terrified of doing anything to compromise that identity. Because if I wasn't a good girl, what was I?

Playing hockey, I found out that good girls had nothing on strong women, on women who *take risks*. Putting my physical body on the line every time I stepped into the game became a tangible reminder that the most exciting things in life don't happen to people who sit on the sidelines.

I started stepping out into the world, unafraid of how it might perceive me. This is not to say that I don't, deep to my core, want to be the best person I can be. It's just that a lot of things—playing hockey, medical school, international travel, motherhood—have expanded my adolescent definition of "good."

Ice hockey taught me that being tough didn't mean you couldn't be kind. My fiercest teammates were also the most loving.

Anatomy lab taught me that the best girls aren't squeamish.

Travel to South Africa made me realize that the best girls aren't afraid to be alone. The medical research I did there taught me not to fear doing something completely different.

My surgery rotation made it very clear that the best girls aren't afraid of being decisive.

My urology rotation showed me that the best girls aren't embarrassed by penises.

My writing groups impressed upon me that the best girls aren't afraid of loud truths.

My children remind me, every day, that there is so much to fight for.

As my definition of "good" expanded, so did my circle of friends. And I realized the most devastating consequence of the model minority myth: how neatly it plays into bigoted myths of traits that are "good" and those that are "bad," and how easily it divides the pie graph of our lives into "us" and "them."

Writing this piece, I've struggled to pinpoint the moment when I realized that my family was more than a little racist. I vaguely remember my father complaining about the "Americans" he had to teach, and I remember the scandalous tone my mother took when she gossiped about one of my cousins dating a "hei ren"—a Black person. But I don't have to look very far to see evidence of the Asian superiority complex in the here and now. I see it in the soft grumblings about affirmative action that I read in online parent groups. I see it in my Vietnamese patient who railed to me about how "those people" don't contribute to our country after immigrating the way that "our people" do.

And so I continue to fight, not only for my children's right to be seen and valued for who they are, but *against* the lifelong sense of entitlement that comes from being a teacher's pet. Being a model doesn't always mean that you're the best, just that you're the most successful at giving people what they expect. I want my children to have the whole world to grow into.

When I got married, it never even occurred to me to change my name professionally. I was always, and always will be, Dr. Wong. It was only when I needed a nom de plume that I took my husband's last name. I still wear it uneasily, like a child wearing a plastic mask with eyeholes that are just a few millimeters off. Because, for the first time in my life, I want people to see me as Asian.

I want them to see me be loud, rebellious, and sometimes profane, and watch their assumptions about the model minority be blown into tiny bits. And at that moment of cognitive dissonance, when their stereotypes are subverted, I want them to remember with a start that we don't yet live in a post-race society, not by a long shot. But our first step is to look beyond our expectations, not just in other people, but in ourselves.

NOT LIKE THE OTHER GIRLS

Martha Brockenbrough

"A woman who is very flat-chested is very hard to be a 10."

–Donald Trump

The first time I took my shirt off in front of a boy who was not a blood relative, he told me to put it back on.

We were in my bedroom. I sat on the bottom bunk, and he looked down at me. "You're a girl. You have to wear a shirt."

I was six years old and he was seven, a friend of my older brother. He wore faded cutoff jeans, and his skin was taut and tanned over his sun-polished muscles. He was one of a pack of boys who roamed the neighborhood riding bicycles, throwing dirt clods, and best of all, playing baseball on the lumpy dirt field near the shopping center. I wanted to join them.

"But I'm hot," I said. "And *your* shirt is off."

I showed him my flat chest. I, too, was muscled, from playing soccer and swimming, though my skin was paler than his,
especially on the parts that were always covered by my clothing.
"We're the same, see?"

"You're a girl," he said. "Girls have to wear shirts because
they have boobs."

I pulled my green cotton ringer close, covering the parts he
was talking about. It was so hot out—the kind of summer day
that draws the sweat out of you and leaves your skin rimed with
salt and dust and your mouth dry and wanting. Going shirtless
as I ran through the rhododendrons at my parents' house made
things a little bit better, but more important, had made me feel
the equal of my brothers and their friends.

I put my shirt back on.

It was the mid-1970s then, and my brothers played baseball on
a team through the local Boys Club. There was no Girls Club
then. That would come later—too late for me ever to play. But
I wanted to.

My older brother was a star athlete. A leftie, he'd stand at the
plate in a pose of fierce concentration, his tongue out. Someone
took a picture of him and printed it large in black-and-white,
making it look like an image from the past, important and true.
I'd hold it by the edges, careful not to mark it with my finger-
prints. I stuck out my tongue to see if that was the magic that

made him such a powerful hitter, the secret that let him snatch a sinking baseball out of the blue with his glove, snapping the leather closed around it.

My younger brother did not stick out his tongue. He was not a great hitter, and the one time he caught a baseball, it was an accident. He'd been daydreaming behind second base, his glove open wide, and a pop fly dropped into it. Roused from his reverie by cheering, he looked all around for the ball, only to realize slowly that he already had it in his hand.

The moment was exciting and hilarious, and he won the game ball, making it one of the best events I'd ever watched from the bleachers, where the moms and sisters sat, knitting, chatting, reapplying lipstick, watching. Once, one of the moms was wrapping birthday presents during a game, and she taught me how to fold the ends of the paper so the lines would be crisp and even, the tape concealed. I did not want to watch, or chat, or learn how to wrap birthday presents. I wanted to play.

There was room for all sorts of boys on the team—boys who dominated, boys who daydreamed. There were cheers for all of them.

There were none for me, although my gift-wrapping skills remain top-notch.

On the first day of first grade, my mother waited with me at the bus stop. When the bus arrived, she nudged me up the steps. I found a seat near the front, and the bus rumbled down the road, smelling of exhaust and the breath of children. I was barely big enough to see out the steamy window, but I knew when we turned left at the intersection instead of right that something was not quite right.

Maybe, I thought, the driver knew a different route to my school. Or maybe there would be two stops.

Maybe.

And then we arrived at the other elementary school in town. I waited in my seat, still hopeful, but the driver told me to get off and go to class.

I slouched off the bus. At the base of the stairs were the hands of grown-ups shepherding kids to their classrooms, but I knew these hands were not for me. I couldn't bear to look at their faces. I didn't want to ask for help. That only would have made things worse. It might have made me cry, and that was out of the question.

I slipped away from the hands and quietly crossed the street, and I walked in the direction of my school. I had new sneakers and my lunch box, and I hustled beneath the green-black arms of Douglas firs and alongside glossy laurel hedges. I knew I'd be late, but perhaps I wouldn't be *very* late.

I made my way along the shoulder of the road, for there was no sidewalk, and a car pulled up alongside me. I pretended not to notice. The driver rolled down the window and called my name. I turned to look. She was the mom of a preschool classmate.

"Do you need a ride?"

I shook my head. It was easier to pretend none of this had happened, easier to pretend I was invisibly unwinding the disaster of the morning by myself. And yet she would not leave me. She drove beside me slowly as I walked, perhaps understanding my need to keep myself together was as important to me as her need to protect me was to her.

The more steps I took, the clearer it became that these two schools were not close together, not close at all. I finally accepted a ride just as a squad car drove by. The police officer followed us to school, ensuring my arrival was the opposite of invisible. When I made it to my classroom at last, my kindhearted teacher told me to sit anywhere.

I chose the table with the books.

"Anywhere but there," she said.

Everyone laughed. My face burning, I chose a regular desk by the blackboard and did everything I could to keep the tears from falling.

After that day I did not ride the bus. They all looked alike. Any one of them could take me anywhere. I wouldn't make that mistake again. I figured that if I could beat the bus home, no one would be the wiser. It was exhilarating to feel my feet against the pavement and to hear the bus far, far behind me.

This is how I became a runner.

In fourth grade, I raced my first 10K, wearing leather Adidas that blistered my heels. My little brother and I finished together. He'd waited for me as we ran up a hill, and I picked him up out of the mud when he slipped near the finish line. Hand in hand, we crossed it.

"You're the next Bruce Jenner," a grown-up told me. Only a few years earlier, Bruce had won Olympic gold medals and appeared on Wheaties boxes. Long before she came out as transgender, she was the athlete the boys wanted to be, the man girls wanted to be with. It was a compliment, and I reveled in it.

The summer after first grade, I took tennis lessons at a court not far from school. To get there, I rode a similar route on my blue one-speed bicycle, which I'd covered in stickers from the Buster Brown shoe store. The route was pretty. It meandered from my evergreen-tree-lined street down a short hill and onto a narrow path alongside the highway. It wasn't far, a mile or so, and I'd ride my bicycle holding the handlebars with one hand and my tennis racket with the other.

One day, as I turned off my street and headed toward the hill, I noticed a car. A small red thing whose make and model I can no longer recall. But I remember its headlights looked like eyes. The car circled back and stopped not far from me. The driver rolled down his window. Sunlight glinted off his metal-rimmed spectacles.

"Do you know where the Turnips live?" he asked.

I knew of no one named Turnip. I did know of the root vegetable, though. I wanted to be helpful, but I didn't know how.

"Why don't you come over to the car," he said. "I'll show you the address."

I went to the car. The man's pants were unzipped. His penis, the first I'd seen that did not belong to one of my brothers, was erect.

"This is a dolly," he said. "Girls like to play with it. Will you play with my dolly?"

A good girl kept her shirt on. A good girl did what she was told. I was a good girl, or at least I wanted to be. So I obeyed. It simply didn't occur to me to say no. When I could bear it no longer, I excused myself. "I have to go to my tennis lesson."

I picked up my racket and my bicycle and I pedaled off, wishing I didn't have to touch the handlebars. My hands had become disgusting to me. But I had a tennis lesson to go to, and I had to get myself there.

I arrived at the court, and dropped my bicycle and racket in the grass by the drinking fountain. I had to hold the faucet for water to flow, so I could only wash one hand at a time. I had no soap, and I couldn't rub my palms together, but this was better than nothing. As I was cleaning myself as well as I could, one of the girls in my class approached. I blurted out what had happened. I can't remember her reply, or if she even had one.

Later that day, when I told my brothers and sisters what had happened, they didn't believe me, and I didn't argue the point. I didn't want it to be true, so why would I? Because my siblings didn't believe me, I didn't tell my parents. I didn't want them to know what I had done.

But the girl in my tennis class told her mother, and about two weeks later word got back to my mom. When she came to pick me up at a sewing lesson that day, her face was gray. I suspected I was in trouble, the worst I'd been in. I said as little as I could about what had happened, and then she dropped it. Afterward, I tried to forget about what happened. I had tried to be a good girl and, in the process, I'd been bad. The worst. This was not a game I could win.

Here is a true thing: no matter how fast you run, you cannot leave your own body behind. The things that happen to your body stay with your body. Cells die and are replaced, but each one of them carries the memory of what happened to the ones that came before. You can sometimes outrun other people. But you cannot outrun yourself.

"You're not like the other girls."

–Gilbert Blythe in *Anne of Green Gables*

This is what I believed: You can't win the game as a girl. But you can become as much like a boy as possible. You can play soccer with the boys at recess. You can become a fierce long-distance runner and swimmer, beating all but the fastest boys. You can be funny. Strong. Competitive. Hilarious. You can wear jeans and sweatshirts. You can cut your hair short.

Then you can grow your hair out again because it turns out it's not all that fun being mistaken for a boy, and besides, you don't want to become so much like a boy that you are no longer wanted as a girl.

You do not yet have the word for this thing you are feeling.

But you can angle for some magic-sounding words that promise to bridge the divide: *You're not like the other girls.*

These words were a compliment. Gilbert Blythe said them in *Anne of Green Gables*, and this was the best thing a girl could be. There are so many ways of being not like other girls. Don't be catty or give the appearance of vanity. Be fast. Be strong. Be good at sports and science. Never cry. Never show anyone you can be hurt.

Because of your body, you must be a girl. But you don't have to be *like* one.

"She runs like a guy," my older brother said.

He was praising one of the stars of our cross-country team, a girl who was a senior when I was a freshman. And even though I often beat her across the finish line, there was apparently something about her that was better than me in my brother's eyes.

I studied her form to understand it. She held her elbows high and out, with her arms at something of an acute angle. They looked like elbows that could do damage to a competitor's ribs. I tried it, but it felt exhausting to run that way, exhausting and untrue to my own natural form, which was efficient and low to the ground. It was tiring and false in the way that taking

AP math and science classes was tiring and false. I was one of the only girls in these classes, and I took them not because I loved them—I loved writing and art and music—but because I wanted to prove that I could keep up with the boys.

Girls can do anything boys can do.

You can do anything a boy can do. I was told this again and again. With every goal I set, keeping up with or beating the boys became my benchmark. I earned a dozen varsity letters in high school. I was the captain of four teams. Along with two boys, I was the editor in chief of the school newspaper, and of our trio, I wrote the hardest-hitting editorials. This was feminism to me. Be like the boys. It was the best way to be a girl.

I competed with the boys, but I wanted to be noticed by them. I wanted to be *wanted* by them, even as I purposely rejected the feminine. I was skinny. Intense. Opinionated. Nearsighted enough to need glasses. And although I cultivated a small group of female friends I loved, I took no particular pride in them.

"Most of my friends are guys," I'd sometimes say. Although this wasn't true, really. They were my older brother's friends, and I had attached myself to this crowd because I could spend time in the company of boys and study them closely, the way a biologist might study captive apes.

The male of the species likes watching horror movies. He demonstrates a rudimentary understanding of physics by shotgunning beer. His games often involve hitting his fellow males in the shoulder for failing to say a nonsense word quickly enough.

One night I fell asleep on the carpet while I was with my brother and one of his friends. I woke up and heard them talking about a girl's body. I had a crush on this friend of my brother, and to hear him talk with admiration about this other girl's curves turned my heart into a pincushion. And then he said, "But don't tell Martha. She'll tell everyone."

This was the moment I knew I'd failed. I wasn't a boy. Nor was I an object of desire. I was a leaking mouth and nothing more. I kept my eyes closed and tried to breathe like a person lost to sleep.

> **"Women can play poker because anyone who can fake an orgasm can raise on a pair of deuces."**
> –Brett Butler on *Grace Under Fire*

Proximity and quiet desperation have their benefits, though. I dated several of my brother's friends. One of these boys was an athlete, with a tanned and muscular body and jet-black hair that framed the edges of his face. In short, he was hot, and it surprised me to no end that he liked me. He once slipped his jacket over my shoulders at the homecoming football game when I looked cold, and months later, as we sat on the bleachers between events at a spring track meet, he told me I was cute.

Just before the school year gave way to summer, we sat side by side in the little room the trainer used to tape up injured athletes. The union of our fingers and palms felt like an event horizon, a point of no return with galactic consequence. Outside observers might see something as benign as two teenagers clasping hands, but inside my soul felt pulled someplace unmapped, even in my imagination. Could someone *really* care about me, despite the many ways I was flawed and broken? Or was he after something else?

That fall, our team had competed in the state cross-country meet. Afterward, exhilarated and silly, a few of us decided to play a game of strip poker on a creaky antique bed in the grand Victorian bed-and-breakfast the team was staying in. The place belonged to someone who taught at the school, and it had been won in a game of cribbage. The winning hand hung on the wall in a frame. It was the sort of thing I'd never seen before and couldn't imagine: wealth that enabled people to bet something as big as a house, and the audacity of the winner taking what he'd been offered, what he'd won, but what was simply too big to be transferred so casually.

I did not win the game.

I lost, with agonizing slowness. And as my clothes came off, piece by piece, I found myself regretting my underwear. Rather than putting on something lacy and daring and desirable—which I'd recently acquired—I'd chosen my most comfortable bra for after the race. A jog bra. I can no longer remember its color, but I liked wearing those because they were streamlined and functional, and they had no cups to remind me of what I lacked. (My breasts were small enough that my parents discussed their size behind my back, and my mom later presented me with their conclusion: I had small boobs because my body fat percentage was low.)

Somehow, just as I had hoped, despite my failure to wear alluring underwear, this boy and I found ourselves in the parlor, a room with French doors and a couch silhouetted in moonlight like some great lounging beast. Despite the presence of the couch, we were on the floor. Or, rather, I was. He was on top of me. I'd put my shirt back on, and he took it off, and then my bra was off, and he was kissing my lips, my neck, my bare flesh, those small breasts that had been found undersized by my own parents.

His hands wandered lower. I pushed them away.

I was not ready for this.

I was a Catholic girl who'd promised to save herself for marriage, if there was anything left to be saved after what had happened with the man in the little red car. It wasn't that I'd thought of that man again, not really. Every once in a while I thought of the glint of sunlight off of his glasses. I thought about the word he'd used. *Dolly.* But most of my energy was spent hiding the broken bits of me.

I had never wanted to be anything but good, and I was not. Every time my parents scolded me, every harsh word I heard, every time I failed to achieve perfection in a world that demanded it: be a girl, but not like the other girls; be like a boy, but not a boy; be the fastest, the smartest, the best . . . By the time

I was that age and on my back beneath a boy, I felt like it was only a matter of time that the rotten truth of me would be laid bare for the world to see, and I would be rejected once and for all.

It was a dark room we were in. But my eyes had long been used to darkness, and I saw everything. That darkness that we fumbled in felt dangerously day bright. I was still the six-year-old who did not want to be seen as she suffered, the one who had to be covered in a shirt, the one who tried to walk an impossible line between masculinity and femininity, the one who had no place in the world where she felt wanted just as she was, except by the cruelest of strangers.

"No," I whispered when he slipped his hand into my pants.

He rolled off me. And he sat there, his edges bathed in moonlight. And then he said good night and walked through the French doors and into the darkness beyond.

I put my shirt back on. I slipped into my room and under the covers, trembling, wondering why on this night, of all nights, he'd wanted to do so much more than we ever had in the past. Had he wanted me? Or had he just wanted sex?

The next morning he stood in the open doorway of the bus taking us home. He glanced down at me and said nothing. He turned his back to me and got on the bus. I sat by myself up toward the front, bewildered and numb.

The next week marked the opening of the season for Tolo, the dance where the girls chose their dates instead of the other way around. Surely he wouldn't have done those things to me if he didn't like me, I told myself. And so I called him on the phone and I asked him if he'd be my date to the dance before it was officially announced.

It was a faux pas, but I needed to know where I stood.

He did not answer directly. I cannot recall the rest of the conversation, or even whether there were more words.

I did not need them, though, to have my answer.

He went to the dance with another girl, an extraordinarily beautiful one with dark eyes and hair, elegant cheekbones curving over dimpled cheeks, and teeth that gleamed like cultured pearls.

He and I never spoke to each other again. I was nothing to him, after all. Just a mouth to kiss on the floor of a grand mansion that was worth less to someone than the thrill of gambling it away.

> **"And when you're a star they let you do it.**
> **You can do anything . . . Grab them by the pussy.**
> **You can do anything."**
> –Donald Trump

A few years later, I was working at a hotel on Crete, a small island off the coast of Greece that I'd first read about in my books of mythology. Crete was home of the labyrinth, a maze built by Daedalus to contain the monstrous offspring of the queen and the bull she loved. As legend told it, a hero named Theseus, with help from a girl named Ariadne, found his way out of the maze.

Theseus later abandoned Ariadne as she slept, and Daedalus's son Icarus flew too close to the sun on wings made of wax and fell to his death in the sea. Crete was a beautiful tragedy, a cautionary tale about love and wishes.

In real life, though, the labyrinth isn't so much a maze as it is a mazelike series of small rooms below the surface of red-gold soil. On the walls throughout the hive of rooms, someone had long ago carved two-headed axes. Labryses. Butterfly-shaped, and symbols of female divinity. These axes gave the space its name.

Outside the labyrinth, archeologists had arranged huge jugs that contained remnants of ancient olive oil. These jugs were called amphorae because they are carried with two hands. That's literally what the Greek word means: "carried with both." The English word "ambivalent" comes from the same root, and it means "bonded to both things."

I was twenty years old that summer, with dark hair that fell below my shoulders. My body was slim, and for the first time since I was four years old, I wore a two-piece bathing suit. The top part fit, which struck me as miraculous enough that I was willing to pay twenty dollars for it.

I spent the summer working there, making drinks for German tourists, clearing tables, washing dishes, and doing whatever else I'd been asked, even as it was not the translation work I thought I'd be doing. I was there, and aimed to make myself useful. I shared a two-room cottage with two women from Denmark. They shaved their crotches but not their armpits, and found it strange that I did the opposite. They also made fun of my pale skin—"You look like milk!"—so I did my best to brown myself up.

During the long lunchtime breaks Greeks take at midday, we'd often go to the beach together. My roommates laughed at me for tanning with my top on. The one time I took it off, an adolescent boy approached me on the pebbled beach, ostensibly to sell me something. His eyes never left my chest. I felt mortified. Dirty. Judged for being too small, too slutty, too something.

The boy was shirtless.

One day during my lunch break, I lay on some flat black rocks by the shore, my eyes closed against the midday sun. I perceived a shadow and felt something metal drag from my navel to my throat. I opened my eyes. Silhouetted against the brazen blue sky was my boss, who was probably in his fifties but seemed to me an old man with his slicked-back, iron-colored hair and his manner of exhaling cigarette smoke with his tongue jutting up and out, like a stone gryphon's.

He was a beloved hero on the island, the kind of man who'd invite priests for dinner and dancing on the balcony as the setting sun stained the Mediterranean red. That metal thing I'd felt sliding from my bikini bottom to my throat was the crucifix that hung from his neck. My eyes went wide. I said nothing. I took myself inside.

Not long after that, he invited me to stay at his apartment in

Athens. He told me not to tell the others, but said I could use it as a base for exploring the mainland. I thought he was being generous, so I took him up on it. I arrived in Athens exhausted from a ferry ride that deposited me at the docks around midnight. He greeted me at the door wearing a bathrobe made of silver silk, embroidered with a Rolls-Royce logo over his heart. The robe was short enough to show the hem of his white underpants.

"Are you strong enough?" he asked.

"Strong enough for what?" I pushed him away, realizing at once how naive I'd been.

The apartment had one bedroom. I took refuge there and barricaded myself in, sliding a honey-colored bedside table in front of the doorway. Through the square glass of frosted window in the door, I could see his silhouette hesitate and then disappear. I slept fitfully in the queen-sized bed, waking up every so often, every time having to remind myself where I was.

The next morning, over a light breakfast, he asked me if it would have made a difference if he'd been his son's age. His son was twenty-three.

He was still wearing the short bathrobe. I couldn't bear to look him in the eye, but I didn't want to look at his bare legs, so I studied the tablecloth, the teacup, the empty bowl of yogurt.

"No," I said. "It would not have made a difference."

I left after breakfast and checked myself into the YWCA on America Street, praying my credit card would go through. Once I had secured a tiny, private room with a twin bed, I went to the

Acropolis, where the Parthenon rose into the blue like the shattered carcass of a once-splendid animal. An Englishman's voice behind me announced, "Prepare yourself for one of the defining moments of your life."

I turned. He wasn't talking to me. He'd taken his wife by the forearm so that he could let her know she was about to be forever changed by this relic of the past. He wore a tan shirt, tan shorts, and a tan hat, and I hated him immediately.

Later, when I went into my boss's office to confront him for what he'd done, he denied everything. I'd misunderstood, he told me.

"What if I told your wife?" I said.

"Let's tell her right now," he replied.

I paused.

Maybe I did misunderstand. Maybe I was being stupid. In any case, I did not want to tell his wife, who had sad brown eyes, russet curls, and the soft body of a woman who'd borne two children, the sort of physique that had inspired sculptors in grander ages than ours. I left his office, doubting myself. Not just my body now, but also my mind.

And yet . . . there was that question he'd asked, in his moment of humiliation: *Would it have made a difference if I were my son's age?*

I should have told him yes.

I've had to prove myself with every job I've ever held, and I thought I'd figured out the formula. It was the same one I'd used all through school. Watch the boys. Watch the men. Be as good or better if you can be.

"What, *you* run marathons?" a male city desk editor said when I mentioned I was training for one. Apparently my body didn't look capable.

"No offense," another male boss told me when I was applying for a job I was amply qualified to do, "but how much experience do you have?"

I had a lot, in truth. I was the editor of my college newspaper and managed a staff of more than a hundred and a budget well over a million dollars. I'd won journalism awards. But no matter what I'd done, it was never enough. Never the right kind. Or I wasn't the right kind of person.

"People like you are a dime a dozen," one editor told me.

And it was true. Print journalism had become a pink-collar job, chock-full of white women who wanted to do some good for the world, to be brave, to ferret out the truth from dark places and bathe the wounds of the world in healing sunlight. Once women decide to do something, the work loses its value.

Here's what I *wish* I'd asked him: *And what about* you—*a middle-aged white man. How much per dozen?*

I didn't even think to ask it, or question for a moment a man's right to succeed. All my life, I'd been watching white boys and white men compete. I tried to make myself into one of them, and while I never wanted to be one, I was ambivalent about femininity. I could see nothing to love about it, even as I wanted to be loved as a girl. And at every step of the way, I learned just how little I was valued. Not for my body. Not for my heart. Not for my mind. All of it was for boys and men to manipulate, and for me to go along with it. I thought I was being a feminist, when in reality I was hating women. And in centering my life around the men who had the power—white men—I was utterly disregarding other women, and particularly women of color, who carry at least twice my burdens.

Sometimes I think I tried so hard to erase this truth of me that I willed myself to have a small chest, the least a woman can have and still be a woman. It didn't make a bit of difference. In every job I ever had, I made less than the man sitting next to me—including the one I married, the one man I decided to believe when he told me he loved me.

It wasn't until we had two daughters that I began to see the world differently. I had no choice in the matter. These girls, one with dark hair and eyes and one blue-eyed and fair, are like suns to me: so beautiful it hurts to look at them. There is nothing wanting about their bodies, their minds, their souls. They do not have to be like boys in any way to generate a force that pulls my heart the way the moon pulls at the earth, invisibly, but inexorably. They are enough, miraculous, splendid, just as they are, for just who they are. I refuse to see them—or any girls—through the warped lens of a world that loves men best.

All girls are as distinct as individual stars in the sky. All girls are also part of the universe's infinite pattern. How wonderful, to be just like all the other girls in this way. How wonderful to be part of this vast and dazzling existence.

The dust of the baseball field is made from the dust of stars. And so are you and I, and this is the truth: each of us emerged from the soft hollows of a single woman who was like no other, and yet like all the others. We are all linked backward through time to the first star that pierced the velvet of night.

Billions of us, and every last one of us full of light so brilliant it stings, if only we are brave enough to look.

IS SOMETHING BOTHERING YOU?

Jenny Torres Sanchez

I was in seventh grade and late for the bus again. I was wearing light pink jeans as I ran across my front yard on a rainy morning, just barely making it on to the bus, and collapsed in my seat. Another fine morning.

When I got to school, my friend yelled, "Jenny! You have a bunch of crap all over your jeans!" She pointed and laughed as others turned to look at me. Sometimes I wondered why that girl and I were friends.

I rushed to the bathroom and saw how splattered and stained my jeans were with mud. I was angry and I started to cry. I didn't like to cry, and definitely not at school. But it was too much, and I guess I cried in a way that my friend knew wasn't really about my jeans.

Later that day, the school guidance counselor called me into his office. It was a small, claustrophobic room. Maybe that was part of the reason I didn't tell him my father was being chased by Ku Klux Klan members. Maybe that's why I didn't tell him that in that very moment, while we sat in his tiny office and he looked at me curiously and asked me questions, a group of men could be beating my father to death.

I sat on a small leather couch.

"Someone said they were worried about you," he said.

My friend who was sometimes mean and sometimes nice came to mind. "I don't know what you're talking about," I said.

"Is something bothering you these days, Jenny? Anything you want to talk about?"

"No."

He tried several times, rephrased questions, tried different angles. But I shot him down each time. And when he told me to please come back if I ever wanted to talk, I knew I never would. I couldn't get out of there fast enough.

In the weeks before I found myself on that leather couch, I sat on the floor of my living room with my older sister and baby brother because my parents had gathered us together. My sister and I exchanged looks. We knew something was up. We'd never been gathered like this before. We didn't have family meetings or family game nights. Something was wrong.

My father looked at us and proceeded to tell us he wouldn't be home regularly. As an interstate trucker who ran routes up and down the East Coast, he was hardly home as it was, but his schedule did bring him home at least a couple days a week. But now, he said, he would be home even less.

"Why?" we asked.

"There's a problem," he said. He didn't want to tell us, but he also needed to explain his absence. He didn't want to scare us, he said, but he wanted to tell us the truth. So, my dad explained to us about the men who were following him. "They tell me they're in the KKK. I think it's better if I don't come home. I don't want them to know where we live. I lose them before I come here, but it'd just be safer not to come home as much. They keep finding me on the road again." I could see him trying to stay strong and calm for us. But underneath it, I saw fear.

I looked at my sister. I always looked to her. And she looked worried.

My dad told us about the trucker who'd been asking for directions over the CB radio in Spanish because he didn't speak English and was trying to find the warehouse where he had to make a delivery. My father had given him directions in Spanish even though some other truckers told him to *Shut up! Speak English! Go back to your own country!* Grown men were upset over my father's kindness and willingness to help. Grown men decided to terrorize him because of it.

Truckers often run the same routes. They sometimes travel together. The men who heard my father were near him. They figured out what truck he was driving, and they began following him, not just that day, but repeatedly. You can't hide an eighteen-wheel semitruck or easily lose someone who is following you. And you can't follow someone very well when you're in a semi, so eventually these men abandoned their own trucks, their own livelihoods, so they could more easily and stealthily play their game and follow my father in cars and vans. I wondered what kind of hate would make you put aside your own livelihood to terrorize someone else. At that age, I had underestimated how much hate people had. I had seen hate in school, sure, but I never felt like I would be killed over it. Years later, my dad told us about the kinds of things they said to him over and over again on the CB radio, the things they threatened to do to him, to his body, to us, his wife and children. For months they did this while we wondered if he was safe. I would sometimes imagine him being cornered somewhere. I'd think of him in his truck, afraid to sleep even after hours and hours of being on the road. Or worse, being dragged from sleep when they finally spotted his truck in a rest area.

My dad grew up with certain notions of how men should be—tough, showing little to no vulnerability or pain or emotion. The only time I had seen him cry was at his father's funeral. And even then, there were only a few tears that slid down his stern, stoic face. But the day he told us about what was happening, my father's eyes filled up with tears. It scared me because it signaled to me the severity of the situation.

"Jenny, is something bothering you these days?" I stared at the guidance counselor's black dress socks and loafers.

"No."

My family was private. I think this is why I didn't say a word to that counselor. My parents had an aversion to sharing any of our problems with anyone else, and so the attitude in my house was always you handle your own problems. I also think the prejudice and hate my parents suffered as immigrants made them raise us to trust only each other. What happened to us and our family was no one else's concern. Maybe I worried that if I told what was going on, it would put my father in more danger. So I kept it to myself.

"Can't the police help?" I remember asking my dad. He shook his head. "They won't do anything, not unless something happens. Besides . . ." He didn't finish or express his distrust of law enforcement, but I sensed it. Besides, they were following him through several states up and down the East Coast and no single police department would be in charge or care much what happened outside their district. Besides, my dad had experienced discrimination from law enforcement already, especially in the Southern states, where he was threatened the most, where these men felt especially emboldened. I remember wondering why my dad was so distrusting of police.

Years after this incident, he would falsely be accused of trafficking drugs among the tomatoes and limes he delivered and he would be hauled away for questioning before ultimately being released. The produce he was hauling would rot and he would not be paid. No lawyer would take his case though they told him it was a clear violation of his rights. Years later, I would watch news clips of Black men being gunned down by police on television and hear people deny there's a problem or that there's a need for police reform.

So I stopped wondering.

"Don't go," I told him. But my father couldn't afford to miss a trip. There were bills to pay. There was produce to be delivered. This was our family's livelihood.

"It'll be okay," he said. "I'll be okay." He smiled, but it didn't fool me.

Every day, for months, between infrequent phone calls in a time before cell phones, I wondered if he was okay. I wondered if they got him. If they cornered him somewhere. If they forced him off the road. If he was in a ditch somewhere. If they would kill him right away or torture him before killing him. I'd learned about the cruelty of the Ku Klux Klan; I knew what they'd done to people. I knew they liked to hide their faces. I learned that sometimes hate and cruelty is flaunted and other times it is carefully covered up.

We'd moved down to Florida from New York two years before my dad was followed by those men. I didn't like Florida once I got here. I wanted to go back to New York and told my dad every chance I could how much I didn't like it. One of the main reasons I didn't like it was that I felt something in the air, something I couldn't name, something that scared me.

When I went into certain stores, I felt it. A thick air, weighty with judgment, discomfort, fear, disgust. It was something I'd never felt before. It made me want to brush at my arms. It made the back of my neck tingle. It made me feel afraid. Ashamed. Hated.

I didn't know it then, but I realized over the years it was racism and prejudice. That's what it feels like. I saw Confederate flags waving from the back of trucks, on T-shirts and belt buckles. Until then I hadn't noticed how some people looked at my parents when they heard their heavy accents and broken English. I wanted to move back to my old New York neighborhood, where my friends were brown and I didn't feel hated or judged or glared at, where my father wasn't in danger or threatened. I wanted to run, to leave. But we stayed.

Those men eventually grew tired of terrorizing and threatening my father. Little by little, it tapered off. Just like that.

They grew tired.

Like little boys who'd lost interest in a new toy. Who decided they were tired and needed to move on to another game.

But they were not little boys. They were grown men. And what they did was not child's play. It was a crime for which they never had to answer. For a long time my father was looking over his shoulder. For a long time I did not see peace in his face. And it was a long time before I didn't worry each time he left for another trip or I could fall asleep without the images of terrible things happening to him.

Over the years, I saw my city change. I saw more people of color when I went to the store. I saw more same-sex couples holding hands. I felt the heavy, thick air of my youth thin out some, and it became easier to breathe. I still see the Confederate flag, but I also see more acceptance and unity. And twenty-eight years later, my city looks and feels different. I like living here. I'm proud to live here.

But that morning after the election.

That morning, the air felt thick again. I felt the staleness of the past find its way back. And I felt betrayed. I had believed in change and thought I'd witnessed it. But I felt deceived. In many ways, I felt like the kid on that couch in the counselor's office.

Is anything bothering you, Jenny?

Yes, something was bothering me!

I'd felt a knot in my stomach for months.

I'd felt impending doom.

I'd feared the worst and it happened.

I felt gutted and without a voice.

I felt small and as if this world did not understand or care about me.

I felt betrayed.

And angry. So angry.

Because wasn't it obvious? Hadn't it been obvious?

It was nationalized on television. Mexican men like my husband, my son, were called rapists by a man who embodies hate. Immigrants like my parents, my grandparents, most of my extended family, were called criminals.

Is something bothering you, Jenny?

And there were people who worshipped and fed off that hate, lots of people. They rejoiced at the way hate spoke, at the assumptions it made, at the way it lashed out with astounding regularity. This hate wore a suit. It came under the guise of success. And the people around him dressed up their hate too. They wore shirts and hats promoting it. They aligned themselves with it and started vocalizing their own hate. They felt empowered. I saw them standing there, behind their leader, on television. I spent a lot of time just looking at their faces. They looked like the mothers who picked up their children at the same school I pick up my children. They looked like men who played with their kids at the park down the street. They looked like teachers. They looked like people who checked out my groceries. Except here, their faces were all twisted up. They were beaming with hate. No, they did not wear hooded cloaks. They made hate look professional and polished and astoundingly normal.

Is something bothering you, Jenny?

Everyday people, all around me. I started hearing more and more excuses for the hate being spewed. I saw some rally around it and others quietly accept it because it would not affect them, or because it was advantageous for them, or because even though they knew it was wrong, it felt good to hear someone give voice to the secret hate they kept in their heart.

I searched the faces of strangers everywhere I went the day after the election. I wanted to catch somebody's eye, exchange a look of understanding. But I felt like no one would look at me.

I felt like nobody cared. I searched and searched for *something*. Grief or hate. Either one. I just wanted to *know*, wanted to *see*, who stood with me and who stood against me. But I saw so much apathy, which only made me feel worse. I wondered if I could read what people saw when they looked at me. A man came into the coffee shop where I sat trying write. He was wearing a Trump shirt. His back was turned to me and I sat there wondering, if he had turned around, would he have glared at me? Or would he not have seen me at all?

For the first time in a very long time, I felt hopeless. The sobering truth sank in. I've gone through difficult times in my life, and the one thing I always held on to was hope. I've always believed in hope. Even during the situation with my father, I had hoped with all my heart it would stop.

But the moment the 2016 presidential election results were official, I felt hope had betrayed me.

The man who was now our president seemed just as dangerous to me as the men who had terrorized my father.

Is something bothering you, Jenny?

Yes. But unlike that day in the guidance counselor's office, this time I will not stay silent.

As I type these words, he is being sworn in. It is a reality I cannot watch. I will instead do something to work against it. I will write this essay for you and hope it awakens something in you. I think others are doing the same. I think so many did not want to see the seedy underbelly of America, the part where

247

racism and homophobia and misogyny and fear of anything different exists. So many people could not understand the way someone could so easily step in and awaken the hate in others. They did not understand that hate has always been there and it was just waiting. For this moment.

But now I am sensing something else, too.

Other sleeping dragons have been awakened.

Social justice warriors.

And they are raging mad and breathing fire.

I have found hope again. I am hoping now. I will continue to hope. But my hope is accompanied by action now. Because I am not helpless. I am not small. And others in this world *do* understand and care about me just as I understand and care about them. I am not afraid to speak now. And so with others, I will unite, in voice, in written word, in petitions and resistance. Together we will hold those in power accountable for their actions and we *will* make them answer.

We will hope.

And we will bring about change.

WHAT I'VE LEARNED ABOUT SILENCE

Amber Smith

When I began thinking about my contribution to this anthology, I thought I knew exactly what I would write about: *rape culture*. This is, after all, an issue I feel so passionately about, and one I have already explored fictionally in my debut novel, *The Way I Used to Be*. And I've had so many incredible, moving, and validating discussions with readers about rape culture and what it means to be a survivor of sexual violence. But the more I wrote the more personal this essay became, until I realized that I couldn't write about rape culture in the meaningful way I wanted to while continuing to exclude my own life experiences. I felt it increasingly important to openly acknowledge that I am a survivor of sexual assault, although I hadn't felt comfortable sharing this publicly up until the writing of this essay.

Part of the reason is that I'm a very private person and it felt too personal to share (and on a practical level I wanted to maintain a clear separation between the fictional world of my book and my real life, as they are two very different entities). But if I'm being honest, I know the other part of the reason is *silence*. Silence is not only an inherent quality of rape culture itself, but in many ways, it has also been a defining force in my life, and it is something that I will probably always wrestle with to some extent.

I grew up in a military family, one that was very much characterized by a stoic, stiff-upper-lip mentality, especially when I was a little kid. There was always love in my family. But there was never a lot of communication. We didn't talk much about our feelings or our problems. Our struggles—both those of my parents and of me and my siblings—were by and large private battles waged in solitude. (In fact, even as I write these words, my own inner child feels a little anxious that I am breaking some kind of unspoken rule encoded in my DNA.)

My father was in the army for more than twenty-five years and my family moved a lot, which particularly affected my older siblings, as I was not in school when we did most of our relocating. My dad served two tours in Vietnam and it would not be until much later that I realized he had been silently struggling with post-traumatic stress disorder for my entire life. At that time PTSD was not something people understood very well, and certainly nobody was talking about it. Looking back, I can see how PTSD influenced everything that went on in my family, keeping our interactions on the surface, often with a forced sense of calmness. It was almost as if we had all learned to build walls around ourselves, stuck in survival mode by proxy. And so we never ventured into the deep end of the emotional pool, but rather, we stayed in the safety of the shallow end, treading water. In fact, much of the closeness within my family didn't happen until we were all adults.

In this environment, I learned early on to be quiet and agreeable. I was taught to not make waves, keep my head down, mind my own business, and turn the other cheek. *Just ignore the bullies and they will go away* was a familiar mantra. My parents were simply giving me the best advice they had in their arsenal, as all parents do. After all, these were the methods that had allowed them to move through their world when they were growing up. But I lived in a different world and I would learn that these methods would not be the ones that were going to work for me. Instead of making me strong and self-sufficient and resilient, as they were intended, they made me feel small and stagnant and uncertain of myself.

From a young age I felt pretty isolated from my peers, which I now know is extremely common, as nearly everyone can relate to the feeling of being alone. But at the time, I thought I was the only one who felt this way. As I entered school I was painfully shy, extremely introverted, and didn't make friends easily. I had health issues and learning disabilities as a child that made me feel like an outsider. But I was sensitive and creative, and found ways to express myself through art, which has always been my saving grace. I often preferred the world of my imagination to reality, and that is where I felt the most comfortable. Out in the real world, I remember feeling like I just plain didn't belong.

I was in second grade the first time I was sexually assaulted by one of my closest friends. It was not only an act of physical violence, but emotional violence, as well. We had been friends for years, we went to school together, played together, and from my perspective, were best friends, which was no small thing for me. We were playing at his house like we had many other times, when this assault happened. It came out of nowhere, and I remember distinctly feeling as if someone else had taken over this boy I knew so well—both his actions and his words seemed to be coming from somewhere else entirely. In retrospect, I believe (though I can't know for sure) the reason it felt as if it was not *really* him is because he was doing to me what may have been done to him, playing something out that actually didn't come from him. Regardless of why it happened, it was a devastating violation of trust and a betrayal of the bonds of friendship we shared.

I don't know why there were not adults there to begin with, but I am thankful that his grandmother suddenly came home during the course of this event, because that stopped the situation from progressing any further. I know that I was visibly upset and shaken by what had happened. Clearly, when his grandmother saw me she must have realized something was not right, but she said nothing. So I ran away as fast as I could. And my friend soon followed behind, chasing me all the way down the street to my house. I'm sure he was trying to prevent me from telling my parents what had happened. I did tell, though.

I think it must have been a difficult thing for my parents to understand, let alone know how to help. I was so used to downplaying everything because that is how my family operated back then. So I'm not even sure I explained the situation fully or gave any real indication of just how severe, distressing, or traumatizing it really was. I'm not sure if they truly comprehended that I *had* in fact been sexually assaulted by my friend. After all, when we think about children being abused or assaulted, we often assume the perpetrator must be an adult, not another child.

There was no further conversation about it, at least not one that happened with me. Perhaps they felt that there was simply not much to be done. I probably seemed "okay" since I didn't know there was another way to behave at that time, and so we all just acted normal, went about our lives, and never talked about again. This must have seemed the path of least resistance, and it is a story I have heard from so many survivors. But acting normal and ignoring what had happened began to make me feel like what happened didn't even matter, like what happened wasn't important. I felt like it was something I should be able to simply let go of and move on from, only I didn't know how. Looking back, I realize what was happening under the surface was that I was beginning to feel like *I* didn't matter, like *I* was not important.

It was several months later when I was assaulted again, this time by the same boy who had gotten away with it the first time, along with another friend of his. This time I did not tell anyone.

We moved to a different state shortly afterward, and by that point what happened no longer felt like something we were just not talking about; it felt like a secret—something I was not *allowed* to talk about. But secrecy breeds shame. And shame is a sneaky, shape-shifting creature that often changes its form and appearance. Sometimes it looks like anger or sadness, even numbness or calmness, and we create many different masks to hide it. My shame morphed into self-blame. For me, this seemed a logical conclusion, as I tried to make sense of my emotions. If I could manage to find a way to blame myself for being assaulted, then at least that meant I had some amount of control over what had happened, which felt a whole lot better than powerlessness. Of course, at the time I couldn't see this internal and faulty logic. But it was then that I reached the point I was able, for all intents and purposes, to move on from what had happened.

But what I moved on to was silence.

This kind of silence is not simply a state of quietness; it is a disavowal, a denial of both the experience and the emotions attached to it, and with that, a forfeiture of healing. This kind of silence is like a cavity, a void that, for me, was ultimately filled with a profound sense of worthlessness. Sometimes when I think about this process of turning toward the silence, I visualize it as a tiny solar system: imagine you are like the sun, the center of your own universe, the protagonist in your own life story. The planets that surround you are the people and the things that happen in your story. But if you create an intense atmosphere of silence around one of these planets, its density grows and grows, until its gravity is so strong that before you know it, this planet is no longer orbiting you; you are orbiting it—it has become the center of everything in your life and you stand outside of it. Like a black hole, maybe you can't even see it anymore, but you can feel it sucking in all the energy and all the light that makes up your life and your identity. The only way to stop it from devouring everything is to confront it.

But it would still be a long time before I was able to do that.

As I got older, and particularly in middle school, I was bullied pretty relentlessly, which is one of the things that made middle school one of the worst times of my life. I often look back on those years and realize how much inner strength I had hidden within myself to be able to make it through without being completely crushed. As an adult, when I speak about the experience of being bullied as an adolescent, I'm often asked, "Why were you bullied?" or "Why didn't you just stand up for yourself?" These are always posed as harmless questions from people who are simply trying to understand, but it implies that many often think that if a child is bullied they must be doing something weird or wrong to incite this behavior, and unfortunately many kids who are bullied feel the same way. For a long time my answer was always a shrug followed by a mumbled "I don't know." But what I have come to understand is that my being bullied had to do with silence. Standing up to a bully may seem like common sense, a given, but not everyone (particularly young girls) is provided this simple message: you are worthy of standing up for yourself, you are capable of speaking up, and you don't deserve to be treated badly. I never learned how to stand up for myself, or rather, I never learned that I *should* or that I had a right to—I was taught to let it roll off of me. In some instances, maybe that is the right course of action. But in chronic bullying, which is what my experience was, it's almost like standing in the rain. You can only let the drops of water roll off of you for so long before it absorbs into your skin and begins weighing you down.

With my personal history of living in the shadow of a parent's PTSD, and my own childhood assaults that I never dealt with or understood, I often picture myself during my middle school years as walking around with a giant invisible scarlet letter on my chest. *V* for victim. I was not a survivor then. Not yet. I was a victim. I felt like a victim. And that's how people treated me. I was an easy target. One of the other major factors that played into the bullying and my low self-esteem was that I had never done particularly well in school. I received a lot of the "doesn't apply herself" or "doesn't work up to potential" comments on report cards, and that was always so upsetting to me because the thing was, I worked *really* hard, yet I skated by as a below-average student through much of elementary and middle school. I received some extra help at school in speech, reading, and math, in addition to the regular classroom lessons. But I was so quiet about my difficulties and didn't test poorly *enough* to actually be diagnosed with any of the common learning disabilities like dyslexia or dyscalculia, processing disorders I would discover later in life I had been struggling with, so I never fully received all the help I needed. It wasn't until seventh or eighth grade when, at last, there was a light at the end of the tunnel. I finally found methods of learning and studying that worked for me; I just had to stop trying to do things the way other students did. I began to excel in school, which was one of the first things to boost my confidence and help me to carve out my own path. This was a big moment for me, perhaps the first step to finding my own voice.

By the end of eighth grade I was on the honor roll, and as I started high school I was doing very well, getting As and Bs. With my increased confidence, I found that I was not being bullied anymore and for the first time in my life I was not so afraid of my emotions. At the same time, I also didn't know how to deal with them, and for several years it seemed that every emotion I experienced came out as extreme forms of panic, anger, or sadness, and rarely anything in between. I was struggling with anxiety and depression (and unbeknownst to me, my own PTSD), not to mention some pretty significant anger-management and self-harm issues that I ultimately had to seek therapy to get under control.

My father had been extremely ill for many years during this time, and in fact nearly died when I was a freshman in high school, due to a long-undiagnosed (and ignored) thyroid condition that was slowly debilitating him from the inside out. I find it telling that the illness that was literally hours away from claiming his life stemmed from the throat area, where our voices are located—the voice that he couldn't or wouldn't use to talk about his own trauma. Thankfully he did recover, but soon after, my parents divorced, and my father remarried less than a year later. This breakup of my family and the abrupt blending of another family that included new stepsiblings caused a lot of turmoil. But looking back I feel like it was also the breaking open of so many of the things that had been kept in the shadows for so long.

I would realize in my high school years, amid all of this chaos and upheaval, a big part of what made my emotions and my experiences even more confusing is that I was also discovering that I was a lesbian, which is something I think I knew about myself even before I had the language to describe it. When I was in high school, LGBTQ people were not widely accepted or even visible, at least not in my corner of the world. I don't remember there being a single out student in my entire school, though we were certainly present. There were also no Gay-Straight Alliances, as are now thankfully prevalent. At the time, I took my cue from earlier experiences to ignore it, to act like it didn't matter, and to remain silent about it. This became another part of my identity I kept largely to myself until college, hidden from my family in particular, until well into my adulthood.

I share this part of my journey because I feel like so many of my experiences have been related: home life, school life, being assaulted, being bullied, being in the closet, and feeling like an outsider. All of those roads lead back to the same place: *silence.* And it is this silence that is at the core of rape culture.

"Rape culture" is a phrase we hear a lot these days, but I wonder if people really understand what it means. It's more than just a theory or an abstract term—it's a lived reality in today's society, where people are taught how not to be victims rather than how not to victimize others. It's a culture that promotes silence, fear, and shame, placing blame on victims rather than perpetrators. People who have been assaulted are often questioned about their sexual histories, whether their assailant was a stranger or an acquaintance, what clothes they were wearing, and the amount of alcohol they may have consumed, as if any of these factors changes or lessens the violation. Rape culture is a way of thinking that trivializes trauma and normalizes abuse and sexual assault as something that is an expected, even accepted, part of life.

I've spent the last couple of years talking with a lot of people about rape culture, and there are some frequent misconceptions that I've encountered. For instance, many people seem to think that rape culture is something that only affects people who have experienced sexual abuse and assault. But that couldn't be farther from the truth. Rape culture is not simply an issue pertinent to survivors, but an issue that affects all people and one that society as a whole must confront. It is an insidious and often covert product of our culture as a whole, one that strips people of their voices and their power. Everyone is complicit in creating and maintaining it, and if it is to ever come to an end, it will require everyone to do so. While its violence may be implicit, that does not make it any less dangerous. It is the ongoing silence and the stigma of shame that feeds rape culture—ending it involves cultivating an equally strong culture of respect, validation, and compassion.

Another important misconception that I'd like to address about rape culture is that it is not only about physical assault or contact. It is also about unwanted looking, unwanted comments, and the judgment of the actions, decisions, and appearances of (usually) women. This would include occurrences such as "slut shaming" and "body shaming," both of which serve to reduce a human being's entire worth down to one criterion: her sexuality. It fosters not only a lack of external support and compassion, but it is so pervasive that it is even internalized as a lack of self-compassion and self-blame on the part of victims, as I felt so strongly in my own experiences, though I didn't know why at the time.

Rape culture is also not a men-against-women situation. Men and boys are also survivors of sexual abuse and assault. And women often play a huge role in keeping rape culture thriving, as there are so many who are reluctant to engage in dialogue about sexual violence, and are even actively involved in the shaming of other women. What I've learned is that women and girls who shame other women and girls often do so because it is the easiest, and sometimes only, way many people can find to distance themselves from the very real fear that they could just as easily be violated, harmed, or judged in the same exact way. It is a painful truth to face, to be sure, but when it comes to silence and rape culture a big part of the issue is disconnection.

The disconnection is not only a lack of verbalization, it is also the lack of reception—even if your story is being shouted for all to hear, it will fall flat if there is no one there to receive the message. It was this disconnection, fueled by fear that prevented any of the adults involved in my assault(s), both my friend's grandmother and even my own parents, to ask the questions that needed to be asked, or to try to understand what had happened. None of the answers would be easy, and would in fact only breed infinitely more difficult questions, but that is precisely why they need to be asked. Dialogue is the only bridge; it is the remedy to this breakdown that rape culture creates in how we relate to one another and how we show empathy for one another's experiences.

It is this echo-chamber experience that I hear about over and over again, in countless messages and e-mails and even in-person stories from survivors who often share their struggles with me. I have never done any type of speaking engagement where someone hasn't come up to me afterward to share their story of being assaulted, shamed, or silenced in one way or another. I think this is because so many people desperately need someone to listen, to care, and to simply believe them. These are women and men, adults and young people, who are not getting that validation anywhere else in their lives, and therefore they are not getting any help to find healing or justice either.

In one of the first public bookstore talks I gave about my book, I referred to my main character as a "victim." I had barely begun speaking before I was interrupted by a woman in the audience, who stopped me and said something to the effect of "you mean 'survivor,'" as if I'd simply used the wrong, politically incorrect word. And I went on to explain that I did, in fact, think "victim" was the right word, and that the story I was telling was the journey of moving from being a victim to being a survivor. This made her uncomfortable, and as I've talked to more and more people about this subject, I've found that it makes a whole lot of people uncomfortable. "Victim" has become a bad word, a shameful word. Of course, no one wants to be labeled a victim. And using the word "survivor" to describe oneself can be, and is, a deeply empowering experience. But if you feel that you're not even allowed to acknowledge that you have indeed been victimized, then all the roads that lead to survivorship are essentially closed off, and you are left stranded and isolated and invisible once again.

"Victim" shouldn't be seen as the bad word we're not allowed to speak, made to carry all of the baggage of violence. This is yet another manifestation of rape culture. Because the terms "victim" and "survivor" are not simply interchangeable. There is a process of healing that has to happen to get from one to the other. And this is an ongoing process, not something you do once and you're better forever. It is something you have to do every single day. Some days are easy, and other days are more challenging; it is not a linear progression. But I have found that a lot of people don't want to hear about the dark days or the times of struggle. They only want to see the strong image of a person who has overcome. The danger in this is that victims—and I mean *victims*—of abuse and assault are made to carry a double burden of shame for feeling like they're doing something wrong when they don't yet embody that empowered image of a strong survivor.

It has often been in those times of darkness, when I felt weak or powerless, that I have found my deep reserves of inner strength, but only after years and years of denying there was ever any pain or violation to begin with. This is one of the major roadblocks that prevented me from healing, and it's an experience I have heard repeatedly, not only from readers, but from some of the people closest to me who are also survivors. This "victim" versus "survivor" terminology is something I've always had trouble with, because, in truth, neither word encompasses the reality. They both limit how we think and talk about violation and recovery.

Rape culture is tricky, as it both wittingly and unwittingly keeps people from realizing their own power and is part of a larger, more nebulous system that is used to keep people in their place, contained in their boxes, closets, and individual fortresses of shame. It is even sometimes perpetuated by people who are only trying to help—for example, the woman who probably felt like she was performing a public service by trying to stop me from using the word "victim." But even that small act in itself is a form of silencing and shaming. Ending rape culture is really about recognizing our humanity and honoring one another's individual experiences. It is about the right to be safe, to be treated with basic dignity and respect, to be heard and seen without judgment, and to feel important, no more or no less than any other person.

I will be honest. Those dark days I mentioned—there have been a lot of them lately. There is a growing dialogue surrounding rape culture that has been taking place in recent years. For example, we've seen public awareness and discussion becoming more active and visible, from the high-profile Steubenville and Vanderbilt cases, to Jon Krakauer's critically heralded book *Missoula*, even in the films *The Hunting Ground* and *Audrie & Daisy*, and the unbelievably weak sentencing of Brock Turner in 2016's Stanford rape case. The dialogue itself is encouraging, but what it is revealing is that justice is not being served, survivors are not being taken seriously, and it seems as though many people in power simply do not think that sexual abuse and assault matters.

During the second presidential debate, I watched then-presidential-nominee Donald Trump stalking Hillary Clinton across the stage, repeatedly telling her, "You should be ashamed," referring to her as a "nasty woman," when just days earlier the recording in which Trump *bragged* and *laughed* about sexually assaulting women and being able to get away with it had been released. Yet there he was telling Clinton *she* should be ashamed. It chilled me to my core. He attempted, and clearly, to some degree, succeeded, in normalizing his hateful, degrading, and violent comments about women as merely "locker room talk," the old boys-will-be-boys defense.

In the weeks that followed, nearly two dozen women from all walks of life came out of the shadows to tell the world that they had been sexually assaulted by Donald Trump—accusations that spanned decades. His response was to call them all liars, threaten to sue them, even claim they were not attractive enough for him to want [to assault]—anything to avoid admitting any wrongdoing on his part. This is nothing new, as we've seen in recent years, but the elevation and legitimization of the shaming and discrediting tactics that are used to keep survivors silent was brought to new proportions in this election. Politics aside, the simple fact that all of this was overlooked, forgiven (though never apologized for), and that he was still able to become president is the epitome of rape culture.

It has baffled and sickened me to witness what has since unfolded, not only as a survivor, but as someone who has watched as so many of my dear friends and loved ones—both men and women—who are also survivors have struggled to cope with recent events. The presidential campaign and election was nothing short of traumatizing. For many of us who felt as though the violence perpetrated against us didn't matter, or that we couldn't find any support, or that no one understood or even cared, it was like watching versions of our own traumas and our worst nightmares being played out on the world stage. These are all experiences that, for many, cause damage that can take a lifetime to heal, yet in one moment all those old wounds were reopened when this admitted sexual predator was handed one of the most powerful positions in the world.

The day after the election I tried not to panic. I tried to remain levelheaded and began thinking about the actions I would take to show my resistance, and I even tried to logically remind myself that all progress comes in cycles of ebb and flow. But later that day, I decided to take my dogs out for a walk, and no sooner was I outside—in my very own neighborhood, just one house down from mine—when I was gripped with an overwhelming sense of fear that rivaled what I felt directly after my first assault more than twenty-five years earlier. I don't even know how I managed to get myself back inside, but I literally did not leave my house again for an entire week. I couldn't. I felt as though I relived every moment of doubt and pain I ever had, reexperienced the worthlessness and the shame I had worked so hard to manage.

Those first days after the election were some of the darkest. But it was also in that time that I once again found the inner resolve to be my own advocate, once again found my voice and held fast to my principles and my own inner truth. To me this process is the true nature of healing and what it really means to be a survivor (of any adversity). It is not about never being scared or feeling hurt again. It is about *allowing* yourself to feel that way, but then also taking the next step to transform those emotions and channel that energy into something productive. Emotions are not bad, even the ones like anger or fear that are often labeled as such. These emotions always come up for a reason, and that is to let us know when something doesn't feel right. Those emotions are what urge us to make a change or do something about the thing that's not right. It is only when we don't or can't do anything that those feelings overtake us and become negative.

It was from this space that I began thinking about *you*, all of the young people I care about and write for, who are witnessing something devastating and deeply confusing happening in the world. I especially thought a lot about the mixed messages you are receiving about tolerance and violence and self-worth. On the one hand you are taught to love and respect one another, taught to honor your differences, and taught that America was built on the principles of equality, liberty, and free speech. These are the values that we're all supposed to be upholding in our lives every day, yet these ideals stand in stark contrast to what we see happening right now.

So to the young adults reading this, what I want you to know is this: Do not be confused—you matter. Your experiences matter. Your voices matter. Violence and violation of any kind is never okay. It is never asked for and never warranted. Power that is gained by disempowering someone else is *not* power at all. Hatred is wrong—it always has been wrong and it always will be. And lastly, you are not alone.

When I was younger I was always seeking external validation—whether this was in academic pursuits, waiting for someone to stand up for me, waiting for someone to ask me for my story, or waiting for someone to assure me that I would still be loved if I came out. But what I found was that no amount of external validation was ever enough. Because I was still standing outside of my experiences, orbiting that old black hole. It was not until I was able to be really honest with myself and *own* my experiences, to be the support I craved, for myself, that I finally understood what true empowerment was. And the other thing I've found is that once I made this internal shift, I did start receiving the external validation I had once coveted, except it didn't matter so much anymore. What mattered was that I knew I had my own back, my own respect, and my own compassion.

While I don't claim to have all the answers about the current state of affairs, one thing I have learned beyond all doubt is that silence is the driving force behind not only rape culture but so much of the pain and ugliness and disconnection in our world today. And this is no accident. This happens specifically *because* our voices are the most powerful things we have, and that is why others will immediately and frantically try to take our voices away by any means possible. But the point is this: they *can't* be taken away. We all have voices and they all count. They are formidable vehicles capable of creating change. Change happens when we speak up and when we listen, when we have empathy and compassion, when we stand up and empower ourselves and others. What happens next is up to all of us; it is what we create together.

BLACK GIRL, BECOMING

Tracy Deonn Walker

This essay was selected from the editor's call for submissions from unpublished writers.

I once was a Girl Scout. Our weekly troop meetings took place in a reserved room on the second floor of a local church. Each time my mother dropped me off at the entrance, sending me away and up the stairs wrapped in the thin but warm cloak of her smile, she must have known that I was the only Black girl in the group. Me? I'd yet to step into that fact. Looking back, this room was almost certainly the first space I'd encountered framed specifically as a site for female empowerment. In fact, that Girl Scouts meeting room may have been the green-vested, badge-bearing, tilled earth within which my own nascent feminist self began to take root. Unfortunately, that particular soil, and perhaps even that particular feminism, has restrictions on what should grow.

One evening the girls in our troop were on the church's playground, chatting on top of the merry-go-round as it spun slowly, in motion only due to someone occasionally dropping a foot to push it along. We were on our own. A group of preteen girls talking and laughing, unsupervised after the troop meeting, while the moms met inside to talk about boring mom things. One of the oldest girls, Lisa, began to gush about a cute boy in her class, and the group, emboldened, picked up her cue and began to share their own stories of junior high romance. No one was *really* going out with anyone, but our daydreams of doing so grew solid, almost real, as we continued to share. Excited whispers and giggles passed from girl to girl as we spun, eager to participate in one of our first experiences of "girl talk." This type of talk, and the nervous release of hushed secrets spilled, made me feel connected to these girls. To my troop. By the time it was my turn, I had been energized enough that I spoke my own secret without hesitation. I told my troop about a boy on my bus that I had been crushing on for months: Cody. Cody who played soccer and liked grunge music. Cody who wore the most in-fashion Adidas jacket of the time. In *green*. Cody who sat at the very front row of the bus and smiled and scowled in equal parts. (This made his thoughts mysterious, I'd decided. And mysterious was attractive.) Cody who ever so casually said "hi" to me in the halls and had no idea that each time he did so my heart began to race against my rib cage. Cody.

As soon as I finished my brief description of Cody, Lisa pounced quickly onto the name.

"Wait, wait. Is Cody white?!" This caught me off guard.

How did she know? Was "Cody" a white boy name?

"Yes." I confirmed that Cody-the-crush was indeed white. Lisa's giggles set off immediately.

She asked us, asked the entire group: "Wouldn't it be funny if Cody and Tracy got together and had babies? Because they'd be 'swirly' like chocolate and vanilla ice cream! Oh my GOD! How funny would that be!"

The troop laughed in unison at the concept, and I'm certain I did too, even as a part of me was mortified. Even as a part of me realized that this space may have been for girls, but not girls like me. This was the first hint of trouble that my desires—my attractions, what I like, what makes me happy—might not be good topics to share in social spaces. This was the first indication that being a Black girl meant treading carefully. This was the first time I realized I might have an identity illness.

I stopped talking about Cody.

I grew up hating Black History Month. I didn't want to hear about George Washington Carver and his peanuts. I knew who Rosa Parks was. I hated hearing about slavery and the Underground Railroad. I didn't care *that* much for Martin Luther King Jr., although I did appreciate his speeches. They were good speeches. I generally liked historical figures, but the famous Black people we learned about each February weren't just historical figures. They were judgmental, needy ghosts. They stared back at me from their photos and from the black-and-white sketches in my history book, demanding that I care. They needed me to care *deeply,* and they knew precisely when I skimmed over their chapters and lives. And they weren't the only ones who watched me carefully during Black History Month. My white classmates eyed every Black kid in the room during those lessons. Sometimes not for anything in particular, I'd guess. Mostly just for big reactions. They wanted to see me respond to a month dedicated to people who looked like me. But there was no room, no space, no way for me to be excited about Black History Month; excitement about being Black is scary to white people; this much I'd learned. I'd always been an observant child. This default setting was less out of shyness than an overabundance of social awareness. I'd noticed that whenever something culturally "Black" entered our social sphere, be it a hip-hop song on the radio or a dance craze, my white classmates who recited the lyrics and knew the dance gained instant cool points. They were superstars. But I have clear memories of my white peers' eyes growing into wide, uneasy saucers when watching Black students do the same. Blackness by way of whiteness was appropriately filtered, but Blackness by way of Blackness was too raw. Uncut. Scary.

I was surviving middle school only by being as barely Black as I could possibly be. In order to blend in, I needed to care about Black History Month exactly as much as my white peers did, which is to say, not very much at all. But this was the one month during the year when everyone around me wanted me to care, *needed* me to. They needed me to know the lyrics and do the dance. But I couldn't do any of those things, and even if I tried, I couldn't do them like the cool white kids did them. Every February I was asked to be Black on their terms, but I was much too white to respond. I hated those eagle-eyed historical figures in the textbooks that had lived through slavery and who, for one month each school year, kept me muzzled and bound and trapped and anxious in ways that they could have never imagined.

Stay neutral. Keep your mouth shut. Don't raise your hand when they do the Black History Month trivia game, even if you know the answer. Head down and it will pass. Every February 1, I attempted to shrink into the tiniest possible speck in the classroom.

One February my seventh-grade science teacher, who had undoubtedly been tasked with weaving Black history into her curriculum in some fashion, started a portion of her lesson with a line like this: "Some people in the 1800s believed that Black people were meant to be slaves or given lower-class jobs because they thought that Africans were too unintelligent to do anything else."

What a bomb she'd just dropped. I prayed that I wouldn't be called on to reply to whatever ridiculousness this well-meaning white woman was hoping to impart. Heads were already turning my way. I remember sinking into my chair. I remember the loud soundtrack of internal groans beginning its loop inside my head.

My teacher continued her speech, and I'll never forget the

self-satisfied and superior tone of her voice as she said the next sentences: "But, everyone, look at Tracy and Latoya! They have some of the highest grades in this class! That idea was obviously racist and not true. Just a stereotype. If it *were* true, Tracy and Latoya wouldn't have such good grades."

Fuck.

Somehow she'd pulled a triple whammy: she'd reminded everyone that we're Black, revealed that we get better grades than other students, and demanded that everyone give us their attention. The first I knew. The second I'd only guessed at, but it's not something you get confirmed in public. Especially in middle school. The last, well, that just countered the very purpose of *all* of my Black History Month evasive maneuvers.

Everyone turned to me, and I immediately shot Latoya a brief look. We weren't friends, but in that moment we understood each other. Her eyes met mine, and we turned in unison to the front of the classroom, ignoring the other glances. Shields up. Don't respond. It'll be over in a couple of weeks. You won't be their designated Black spokesperson anymore. At least until next year.

Did my teacher really need to rely on Latoya and me to help prove her point? Could she not have sought out *any* other evidence that Black people weren't morons? Did she—did anyone—have lower expectations of me at the beginning of the school year because of my skin? Had anyone in the room been surprised that I was smart?

There was a lot of room in the silence that filled the air after this "lesson." Just not room enough for me.

Always, as the month of February began, anxiety trickled in like smoke under a closed door. By the time we'd hit the second or third week, I'd find myself sitting stock-still in my chair, jaw tensed, heart racing as we learned about slavery and peanut butter and traffic lights and sit-ins. I wanted to run. I wanted to explode. I wanted to claw at my face and skin. It gets like that when you're trying so desperately to pass and the world won't let you, no matter where you go.

I didn't realize how visible my reactions were until one year a friend reached out and tapped my trembling shoulder during a screening of a film about civil rights.

"Are you okay?" he asked.

"This isn't me," I said back through clenched teeth.

I was one of those suburban kids who grew up playing competitive soccer for years in rec leagues. I was an only child, but my mother had to upgrade to a minivan just so she could cart all of my stuff around each week for practices, each weekend for games, and every few months for tournaments. And, of course, so that she could keep up with the frequent demands of carpooling.

Every Sunday morning that we didn't have a game my mother would drag me early to our practically all-Black church for youth Sunday school. I am not a morning person, and Sunday school seemed more like a social experiment than an opportunity to learn about God, but I was also a middle schooler who thought weekends were supposed to be about soccer, reading books, and writing fan fiction, so my perspective was undoubtedly skewed. None of the other kids in Sunday school went to my actual weekday school. I think my mother hoped that going to a Black church on the weekends would help take care of my cultural education on Blackness, an education that I wasn't getting during the week. Possibly an extra hour of Sunday school each weekend with my Black peers would really help that tutoring take. "School" was in the name, but it didn't feel like an education. It felt like a prescription.

This particular Sunday the group of a dozen or so teenagers was seated at a table and our teacher was leading us in a discussion about free time—how we use it, how it can be in service to God, and the role of hobbies in our lives. One girl raised her hand to list the type of free time activities that she thought were *against* God. An oddly critical way into the discussion, I remember thinking. A chief category of concern for her was music and her specific example was a Nirvana song with typically grungy, screamy, ragey lyrics. The room nodded solemnly; this was clearly against God. I looked around the table and guessed (correctly, I'd wager) that none of the other Black teenagers in this room had ever listened to Nirvana on purpose or long enough to learn the lyrics. I had. I liked them. I thought about speaking up and offering a counterargument, citing another example of lyrics from the then-alive Kurt Cobain, but I didn't. I'd recently made the mistake of turning the volume up on the radio when a Smashing Pumpkins song came on. A family member had turned to me and said, "You listen to too much white people music." It had been a harsh diagnosis.

The discussion turned again to the best ways for teenagers to spend free time. This time the teacher spoke to us about the value of athletics in keeping our bodies, our temples, healthy and active. A boy sitting next to me turned and asked what sport I liked.

I answered without thinking, "Oh! I play soccer. I love soccer!"

"'I love soccer!'" He mocked me, voice high and overly enunciated, affecting a hard *r* to the end of the word "soccer." His shoulders shook as he exclaimed, pointing at me. "You sound like a white boy! 'I love soccer . . .'" He was laughing too hard to continue the conversation, but I already knew it was over.

I didn't talk about soccer to Black people again.

When Kurt Cobain shot himself, I brought it up only with my white friends at school.

My unrequited love for white boys continued throughout middle and high school. After Cody, there was Jack. After Jack, Tyler. After Tyler, Bryce. I pined after them just as any awkward teenager pines after their crush, but by eighth grade I knew without asking which ones would never, could never, see me as a romantic interest. For some reason I pined after those boys the most. Even though I didn't think it would magically change my situation, I'd study the girls my crushes dated as if they were beautiful animals in the wild. I'd look for common traits: the brands on their jeans, the words they said, the way they held their backpacks. I couldn't adopt their pale skin and eyes, but maybe I could learn enough to . . . something. I even tried mimicking their hand gestures and ways of speech. Sometimes they studied me, too.

One day at recess I was chatting with a popular girl named Brittany (who was also my friend. Mostly. Sometimes) and she suddenly reached out to touch my hair.

"Your hair is so . . . fun," she said, gazing at it with wide blue eyes. "The way it sticks up and just stays." Brittany was popular because she was very pretty and very nice to everyone. She had straight blond hair and smiled with so many dimples you couldn't count them.

"I guess so," I said quietly. Her hands were still in my hair, tugging on it and playing with the chemically straightened dark strands. I wanted to extract my head from her reach, but I didn't want to seem rude; she was popular and nice.

"I think it's really . . . cool," she said thoughtfully. Brittany was so kind that when her tone went from overly positive to neutral, as it had just then, you knew she must have been thinking something less than kind but was too polite to say so.

She withdrew her hand and wiped her fingers on her pants. The white girls who touched my hair and its oils without asking always wiped their hands on their pants afterward. Like what

I had, what my hair had, like my Blackness was contagious. I know now that they had been rude to touch me and comment on me without invitation, but that knowledge could never work itself past my shame.

By high school my hair had been straightened for so long that I didn't really know what my natural hair looked like. I just knew that the curls, like weeds, needed to be caught early and fought back. My mother drove me once a month for this gardening. At sixteen I could go to the salon by myself, and so I sat one Saturday, watching in the mirror as Pam, my stylist, processed my naturally curly hair so that it was straight. She pointed to the way that my hairline drew down into a point high on my forehead and said, "You have a widow's peak."

"Oh, yeah," I replied. "We learned about these in science class. They're genetic." I smiled, proud that I'd retained that knowledge and could share it.

Pam smile-grimaced back at me in the mirror and *tut-tut*ted. "They mean you have some white people in you."

I'm ashamed that it felt like a compliment as much as an insult. I think she meant it both ways. It didn't matter what her intentions were, though, because it was a reminder of what I already knew. Had already learned. My body's Blackness needed to be controlled or converted to whiteness as much as possible, but I also needed to be Black enough, which I wasn't. I didn't really know which ways of being were most important, but I knew that sitting in that chair was my race ritual. When she was done with my hair and I stood up to leave, Pam always beamed at me as though I'd been cured.

I had my pick of the universities I applied to, thanks to great grades, a fantastic high school education, and superb letters of recommendation. My teachers loved me, even if they sometimes pointed out that I was "quiet" in their classrooms. Their semi-frequent encouragements to "speak up more in class" couldn't compete with the years of social silencing I'd experienced, or the internal voice that policed my body, words, and interests. A "drop in the bucket" would be an exaggeration of the impact of their suggestions.

I went to college with my omnipresent diagnosis of racial unwellness and conflict of womanhood, just as I went to college with AP credits and a new set of Bed Bath & Beyond twin long bedsheets. I went to college smart and quiet.

But school brought me new language. New language brought new ideas. And new ideas led me to new people. I gravitated toward artists and creatives because they celebrated the unknown and the surprising. They spent hours trying to capture the misunderstood. And they encouraged me to make art.

The thing about making art, and writing in particular, is that it demands honesty. Art doesn't want your lies or your armor. Art wants your bloody truths. A blank page wants to be filled. It doesn't judge what you write down. And so I started to write down my identity confusion. I wrote down my frustrations. I wrote down my dis-ease. I wrote my longing. Poems are especially welcoming to the small experiences that feel like violence.

It just so happened that my artistic community included spoken word poets and performers. I'd written poetry and even read it out loud, but never thought of myself as a performer. I knew nothing of "slams." I eventually ventured onto the stage with other people's words, and that felt exciting and bold. It felt like I was spinning. Like the merry-go-round again. Except this community, this group, these audiences, they wanted my secrets. Their kindness was more than the simple absence of cruelty.

I took classes on cultural studies and poetry by women of color. I devoured Cherrie Moraga and Gloria Anzaldúa's *This Bridge Called My Back*, because the women in that anthology spoke of living in "the borderlands." Living in the in-between and the fuzzy cracks within feminism and racism and oppression and spiritual survival. They lived in the racial nowhere that I grew up in and somehow, miraculously, spoke from that space. The space that had taken so many words from me.

I wondered if I could write from the in-between too, and, ever the good student, I asked my mentors for advice. Some of my professors urged me to write about the Black Diaspora, but the old specter of Black History Month rose inside my chest. (*Am I this? Is there room for me here? This isn't me.*) Others suggested that I refer back to key sources and figures in the canon. I looked there to see if I could fit, but I didn't see anyone who wrote about what I knew of performing race poorly. I didn't see anyone writing about the particular type of social shrinking and cultural bending that I'd experienced growing up. About how being brown is not enough to be Black. I found amazing essays by critical race theorists, post-colonialists, and gender theorists, but while our symptoms were similar, our conditions were not. The more I looked for a lineage, the more I felt like a faulty clone. I felt lost again. No one seemed to have the same identity illness diagnosis that I did.

Eventually, I went back to the page that didn't judge and wrote about the quiet intersectionality that lives within my body. You see, because I am a woman of color, I walk around holding conflicts of desire and belonging. I attempt to squash my given self and the things that grow out of my control, like love and curly hair, before they betray me. Sometimes, inadvertently, I nurture those wildlings within. But I cannot eliminate them, either through constraints or encouragement.

I was twenty-one and a graduate student at the end of a week-long intensive performance workshop when I found my freedom and birthed my own Black womanhood. Ten students, including myself, had signed up to form an ensemble who would write and produce original work in a culminating performance for the university community at the end of the week. We endured hours-long writing exercises each night and produced short per-formed pieces each day. We got little sleep. It was artistic boot camp and it was brutal; the pace didn't allow for reflection and so, inevitably, truest selves rose to the surface. By the fifth day, both my writerly voice and my physical voice were raw, and so was my work. I was tired, but my work felt electric.

We were writers and directors of our own pieces, and could recruit other performers as supporting cast members when needed. When I told my friend Josie, who was white, what I wanted her to do to me, she balked.

"Um. I mean . . . I don't know if I can do this. I feel really uncomfortable," she said. My art was frightening her.

I asked her again, pleading. "It's important to me," I said. She relented. She'd seen my process all week. She knew where I was going. And she knew why.

The theater was standing-room only the night of the final performance. I'd never seen our space so packed. People were on the floor in rows, cramped into chairs two-on-one, creating heat and buzzing energy by their presence. I'm pretty sure it was very against fire code. We each performed in turns, and then my piece was up. I had gained new words, as I've said, and so my poetry was both academic and anecdotal. It was personal and it was critical. I spoke about being far too white to be Black while being far too brown to be white. I talked about the panopticon of race—walking with my white friends past groups of Black students gathered together on the university commons and feeling them eye me. I talked about being squeezed by expectation until I was folded in. I talked about listening to and loving Huey Lewis and the News and not knowing much about rap (that got lots of laughs). I talked about being called an Oreo. Dealing with my hair. My white-people widow's peak. At the end of my poem, I dropped to my knees, held my hands behind my back, and installed a blank stare on my face. The rest of the piece would take place in complete silence.

Josie appeared then, circled me, and pulled back on my hair. She pointed at it and then gestured to the audience to invite them to inspect the strands. She pulled back on my lips to show them my teeth. Yanked my arms up high, jabbed at me to make a muscle so they could see my strength. She pranced happily from one side of me to the other, grinning as she showed off my features for the audience's consumption. Showing them the violence of accumulated microaggressions. Of the constant Otherings and Not Enoughs. Of the Why Do You Like Thats. Of white hands in my hair and on my face and Black bodies pointing and laughing.

I heard gasps in the darkness as my imagery hit home. Two hundred people in stunned silence. I was shaking.

Afterward, the audience approached us hands-first. Artists and teachers and fellow students reached for my arms and face. Reached *for* me. Some people had tears in their eyes. I don't remember the words they said, but I remember the hugs. The warmth of a palm on my back. Someone clasped my hands in both of theirs, but they weren't there to inspect. They just held on. Held me. They didn't have the words for feedback and didn't offer any. Every look, every smile, every hug spoke of gratitude. So many people thanking me. People saying and whispering, "yes." I didn't realize that I'd asked a question, but the faces were nodding in answer, "yes."

I've been in dozens of productions since then and seen multitudes more, but I'll never forget what art gave me that night. I'll never forget that art allowed me to redefine the terms of engagement and to fill in the gaps where other people's words and actions had left me without anchor. I may not belong everywhere, but art, and artists, had said yes to my anger and to my fear and to my resistance. Art had made room for me.

Growing up, my identity existed outside of the borders of expectation and so it was me who was diagnosed as unwell. I know now that I am not responsible for living within the limited imaginations of others, nor am I insufficient because they cannot fully conceive of me. I know this because art once whispered, then yelled, then roared through me that it is the world that might be ill and that I am becoming whole.

RESOURCES

Register to vote: www.vote.org

Find your Representative in Congress: www.house.gov
/representatives/find/

Find your State Senators: www.senate.gov/senators/contact

RESOURCES FOR ACTIVISM:

Database of Student & Youth Activist Organizations:
http://www.speakoutnow.org/resource/links-youth-and
-student-organizations

SpeakOut—The Institute for Democratic Education and Culture:
Dedicated to the advancement of education, racial and
social justice, cultural literacy, leadership development,
and activism.

The Youth Activism Project:
youthactivismproject.org
Download the free "Youth 26% Solution" guide to youth
activism: http://youthactivismproject.org/youth-strategies/

Amplify Your Voice (A Project of Advocates for Youth):
www.amplifyyourvoice.org
A website by and for youth and youth activists, focusing
primarily on reproductive and sexual health and rights of
young people.

RAINN (Rape, Abuse & Incest National Network):

https://www.rainn.org/student-activism

Resources for activism around sexual assault prevention and education, from the nation's largest anti–sexual violence organization.

5calls: 5calls.org

Website and phone app to make calling your representatives about the issues you care about easier.

Daily Action: dailyaction.org

Sign up for daily action alerts.

Indivisible: www.indivisibleguide.com

A practical guide for resisting the Trump agenda. Former congressional staffers reveal best practices for making Congress listen.

ABOUT THE AUTHORS

"NOT LIKE THE OTHER GIRLS" by Martha Brockenbrough

Martha Brockenbrough is a Kirkus Prize finalist for her young adult novel *The Game of Love and Death*. She teaches at the Vermont College of Fine Arts and lives in Seattle.

"ROAR" by Jaye Robin Brown

Jaye Robin Brown has been many things in her life—jeweler, mediator, high school art teacher—but recently she's taken the plunge into full-time writer life. She's a Southerner at heart, by way of Alabama, then Atlanta, and for many years just outside of Asheville, but now she's moved north to the great state of Massachusetts. Her debut novel, *No Place to Fall*, was released in 2014, followed by a companion novella, *Will's Story*. *Georgia Peaches and Other Forbidden Fruit*, released in 2016, was named a 2016 Kirkus Best Book and a 2017 ALA Rainbow List Book. www.jayerobinbrown.com

"CHILLED MONKEY BRAINS" by Sona Charaipotra

Sona Charaipotra is a journalist and author who's written for everyone from the *New York Times* to *Teen Vogue*. She's the co-author of the dance drama *Tiny Pretty Things* and its sequel,

Shiny Broken Pieces, as well as the forthcoming *The Rumor Game*. The co-founder of CAKE Literary, a boutique book packager with a decidedly diverse bent, she spends much of her time poking plot holes in TV shows like *Riverdale*—for work, of course. She's a proud We Need Diverse Books team member. Find her on Twitter @sona_c, or on the web at www.sonacharaipotra.com.

"EASTER OFFERING" by Brandy Colbert

Brandy Colbert is the author of the young adult novels *Pointe*, *Little & Lion*, and *Finding Yvonne*, as well as short stories and personal essays published in various anthologies. She lives and writes in Los Angeles. Visit her at brandycolbert.com.

"MYTH MAKING: IN THE WAKE OF HARDSHIP" by Somaiya Daud

Somaiya Daud was born in a Midwestern city and spent a large part of her childhood and adolescence moving around. Like most writers, she started writing when she was young and never really stopped. Her love of all things books propelled her to get a degree in English literature (specializing in the medieval and early modern), and while she worked on her master's degree, she doubled as a bookseller in the children's department at Politics and Prose. Determined to remain in school for as long as possible, she packed her bags in 2014 and moved to the West Coast to pursue a doctoral degree in English literature. Now she's preparing to write a dissertation on Victorians, rocks, race, and the environment. *Mirage* is her debut, and is due from Flatiron Books and Hodder & Stoughton in spring 2018.

"UNEXPECTED PURSUITS: EMBRACING MY INDIGENEITY & CREATIVITY" by Christine Day

Christine Day (Upper Skagit) is a writer and filmmaker. She earned her master's degree at the University of Washington, with a thesis on extinct dog breeds, ancient weaving technologies, and the resilience of Native culture bearers. Her debut middle-grade novel—the manuscript she refused to give up on—is due from HarperCollins in 2020. Christine lives in the Coast Salish region.

"TRUMPS AND TRUNCHBULLS" by Alexandra Duncan

Alexandra Duncan is an author and librarian. Her YA sci-fi novels *Salvage* (2014), *Sound* (2015), and *Blight* (2017) are available from Greenwillow Books. Her short fiction has appeared in several *Year's Best Science Fiction & Fantasy* anthologies and *The Magazine of Fantasy and Science Fiction*. She loves learning new things, from pie-baking and leatherworking to gardening and rolling sushi. She lives in the mountains of Western North Carolina with her husband and two monstrous cats. www.alexandra-duncan.com

"TINY BATTLES" by Maurene Goo

Maurene Goo grew up in a Los Angeles suburb surrounded by floral wallpaper and piles of books. She is the author of the YA novels *Since You Asked*, *I Believe in a Thing Called Love*, and *The Way You Make Me Feel*. She also has very strong feelings about tacos and houseplants. You can find her in Los Angeles with her husband and two cats—one weird, one even more weird. maurenegoo.com

"DREAMS DEFERRED AND OTHER EXPLOSIONS" by Ilene (I.W.) Gregorio

Ilene Wong (I.W.) Gregorio is a practicing surgeon by day, masked avenging YA writer by night. After getting her MD, she did her residency at Stanford, where she met the intersex patient who inspired her debut novel, *None of the Above* (Balzer & Bray / HarperCollins), which was a Lambda Literary Award Finalist, a *Publishers Weekly* Flying Start, and optioned for a TV series by Lifetime. She is a founding member of We Need Diverse Books. Find her online at www.iwgregorio.com, and on Twitter, Tumblr, Facebook, and Instagram at @iwgregorio.

"AN ACCIDENTAL ACTIVIST" by Ellen Hopkins

Ellen Hopkins is a poet and the award-winning author of twenty nonfiction books for children, thirteen bestselling young adult novels, and three novels for adult readers, with more on the way. She lives near Carson City, Nevada, with her extended family, two dogs, one rescue cat, four aquariums, and two ponds (not pounds!) of fish.

"THESE WORDS ARE MINE" by Stephanie Kuehnert

Stephanie Kuehnert is the author of the young adult novels *I Wanna Be Your Joey Ramone* and *Ballads of Suburbia*. She has been a contributing writer to *Rookie* magazine since its launch in 2011. Her essays for *Rookie* and her teenage years making punk-rock, feminist zines inspired her next project: a zine-style YA memoir that will be published by Dutton Young Readers. She lives in Seattle, Washington, and can be found online at stephaniekuehnert.com.

"CHANGING CONSTELLATIONS" by Nina LaCour

Nina LaCour is the nationally bestselling and award-winning author of five young adult novels: *Hold Still, The Disenchantments, Everything Leads to You, You Know Me Well* (cowritten with David Levithan), and, most recently, *We Are Okay*. She lives in the San Francisco Bay Area with her wife and daughter.

"HER HAIR WAS NOT OF GOLD" by Anna-Marie McLemore

Anna-Marie McLemore was born in the foothills of the San Gabriel Mountains and taught by her family to hear la llorona in the Santa Ana winds. She is the author of *The Weight of Feathers*, a finalist for the 2016 William C. Morris YA Debut Award, and 2017 Stonewall Honor Book *When the Moon Was Ours,* which was long-listed for the National Book Award in Young People's Literature. Her latest is *Wild Beauty*, and *Blanca & Roja* is forthcoming in fall of 2018.

"MY IMMIGRANT AMERICAN DREAM" by Sandhya Menon

Sandhya Menon is the author of *When Dimple Met Rishi* (Simon Pulse/May 30, 2017) and a second YA contemporary coming in the summer of 2018. She was born and raised in India on a steady diet of Bollywood movies and street food, and pretty much blames this upbringing for her obsession with happily-ever-afters, bad dance moves, and *pani puri*. Sandhya currently lives in Colorado, where she's on a mission to (gently) coerce her family to watch all 3,220 Bollywood movies she claims as her favorite. Visit her on the web at www.sandhyamenon.com.

"IN OUR GENES" by Hannah Moskowitz

Hannah Moskowitz is the author of over a dozen works for children and young adults, including *Teeth, Break* (a 2010 YALSA Popular Paperback for Young Adults), and *Gone, Gone, Gone* (a 2014 Stonewall Honor Book). She's also the co-author of *Gena/Finn* with Kat Helgeson. For more, see hannahmoskowitz.com.

"FAT AND LOUD" by Julie Murphy

Julie Murphy is the #1 *New York Times* bestselling and award-winning author of *Ramona Blue, Dumplin'*, and *Side Effects*

May Vary. She lives in North Texas with her husband, who loves her; her dog, who adores her; and her cats, who tolerate her. When she's not writing, she can be found reading, traveling, watching movies so bad they're good, or hunting down the perfect slice of pizza. Before writing full-time, she held numerous jobs, such as wedding dress consultant, failed barista, and ultimately librarian. Learn more about her at www.juliemurphywrites.com.

"FINDING MY FEMINISM" by Amy Reed

Amy Reed is the author of the contemporary young adult novels *Beautiful, Clean, Crazy, Over You, Damaged, Invincible, Unforgiveable,* and most recently, *The Nowhere Girls,* about three misfit girls who start an underground movement to avenge the rape of a classmate and overthrow the misogynist culture at their school. She is a feminist, mother, and quadruple Virgo who enjoys running, making lists, and wandering around the mountains of Western North Carolina where she lives. You can find her online at www.amyreedfiction.com.

"THE ONE WHO DEFINES ME" by Aisha Saeed

Aisha Saeed is an author, mama, lawyer, educator, and maker and drinker of chai, as well as a founding member of the nonprofit We Need Diverse Books. She is also the author of the young adult novel *Written in the Stars* (Penguin/Nancy Paulsen Books,

2015) and the forthcoming middle grade novel *Amal Unbound*, to be published in 2018 with Penguin/Nancy Paulsen Books. You can follow her on Twitter at @aishacs.

"IS SOMETHING BOTHERING YOU?" by Jenny Torres Sanchez

Jenny Torres Sanchez is a full-time writer and former English teacher. She was born in Brooklyn, New York, but has lived on the border of two worlds her whole life. She lives in Orlando, Florida, with her husband and their children. For more information about Jenny and her books, visit her online at jennytorressanchez.com or on Facebook and follow her on Twitter @jetchez.

"WHAT I'VE LEARNED ABOUT SILENCE" by Amber Smith

Amber Smith is the *New York Times* bestselling author of *The Way I Used to Be* and *The Last to Let Go*. Fueled by a lifelong passion for the arts, story, and creative expression, Amber graduated from art school with a BFA in painting and went on to earn her master's degree in art history. She grew up in Buffalo, New York, and now lives in Charlotte, North Carolina, with her two dogs. Visit her online at AmberSmithAuthor.com.

"BLACK GIRL, BECOMING" by Tracy Deonn Walker

Tracy Deonn Walker is a North Carolina-based author, scholar, and geektivist. Her master's degree culminated in a thesis and stage play about Superman, West African myths, and secret identities. Fueled by caffeine and a passion for storytelling, Tracy has written and directed theater, produced video games, and taught elementary, middle grade, and undergraduate students. Tracy moderates and speaks on panels about fiction and media representation at science fiction and fantasy conventions. In 2017 she was named a fellow in Duke University's Story Lab and was invited to contribute to *Women Write About Comics*. Tracy can be found at tracydeonnwalker.com.